Joy
to the
World

**A spiritual focus for
personal or group use**

A 31-DAY ADVENT GUIDE

DAVID COFFEY

Contents

Introduction

To be in Bethlehem during the Advent season is a memorable experience. It was my privilege to make a pilgrimage to the birthplace of Jesus in December 2006.

In company with some friends, I made the pilgrimage to show solidarity with the beleaguered Christian communities in both Jerusalem and Bethlehem. Without question it was the most meaningful preparation for Christmas I have ever experienced. Reading familiar passages of Scripture and singing carols in the Church of the Nativity in Bethlehem is something I will never forget.

The raw-edged harshness of modern-day life in Bethlehem stripped away the chocolate-box Christmas we often create in our Advent celebrations. I encountered the wall and the high levels of security, the harsh reality of unemployment, the buoyant faith and vibrant service of the Palestinian Christians of the West Bank, the mixed emotions of joyful hope in the Lord as well as anger and despair at the prevailing climate of violence and hatred. This was the town where Jesus was born. Paul memorably described the event: '... when the time arrived that was set by God the Father, God sent his Son' (Gal. 4:4, *The Message*).

This was my unique Advent preparation on one occasion in my life, but you don't have to be a visitor to Bethlehem to prepare for the great celebration of Christmas. Our lives are probably busier during Advent than at almost any other time of the year. I know the pressures of preparing for and attending school Nativity plays, the extra choir rehearsals for the Advent services, preparing the annual Christmas card list, making arrangements for family gatherings, the delight (or chore!) of choosing appropriate gifts for family and friends. With all this extra activity in the month of December, the thought of 'taking time out' to reflect on the meaning behind our celebrations may seem a luxury. Advent preparation, however, can be as richly rewarding as a well-prepared Christmas meal. It combines devotion, discipline and creative imagination. When we *devote*

ourselves to prayer and reflection, God does surprise
us with new insights within the familiar Advent story.
When we *discipline* ourselves to make time for God in
one of the busiest seasons of the year, we are given the
spiritual power to go deeper in wonder at the mystery
of the incarnation. And when we stimulate our *creative
imagination*, we are led to contemplate the Advent story
through new windows of understanding.

One of my favourite Advent books is *Christmas with
Dietrich Bonhoeffer*.[1] In his opening lines, Bonhoeffer
reminds us that if we want to be part of the Christmas
story we cannot just sit like a theatre audience and enjoy
the play. Instead, we have to be caught up in the script.
We must become actors on the stage, for in this greatest
of all human dramas, each one of us has a part to play.
Advent is the recurring invitation to step into the story and
play our part in the unfolding drama of salvation.

We are created to indwell the biblical story. As we
contemplate the ancient words of our faith, the familiar
Advent story shapes us inwardly and enables us to see
more clearly how we can serve God in our time.

So, we can walk with Abraham, the father of the faithful,
and feel the eternal promise of God: 'Through your faithful
life I will bless the nations of the world.'

We can step into the shoes of Ruth and David, ancestors of
Jesus, and with them sense the destiny of God on our lives.

We can sit with his mother Mary, faithful disciple, and
ask for strength to echo her prayer, 'May it be to me
according to your word.'

We can journey with the Wise Men and pray that some
of our friends who as yet do not follow Jesus will one day
be surprise guests at the stable.

In other words, the invitation is to join the cast! God
has written lines for us in the story of salvation history. As
disciples of Jesus we are invited to contribute a chapter to that
story, and this Advent we can add some pages to that chapter.

1. Dietrich Bonhoeffer, *Christmas with Dietrich Bonhoeffer* (Minneapolis:
Augsburg Fortress, 2005).

How to use *Joy to the World*

This Advent book takes the theme of joy which is so
central to the Christmas message. It has been designed
for personal devotions and corporate worship in the five
weeks of December. I have in mind that those leading
worship will take the main theme suggested for each
week to use in their Sunday services, and that during the
week the theme will be unfolded in daily readings for
personal use.

At the end of each week's readings, I have included
a group activity which could be used by those meeting
for coffee mornings or evening house groups. The final
group activity would be ideal for a New Year's evening
gathering. Some of the weekly group work will require
careful preparation, so it is best to review and prepare for
these projects well in advance!

In Week One the theme is 'World of Joy', when we
consider God's plan of salvation to bless the nations.
Beginning with a look at Malachi's prophecy, we then
trace the family tree of Jesus from Abraham through
people such as Ruth and David.

In Week Two the theme is 'Community of Joy', when
we will reflect on the opening chapters of Luke and some
of the faithful believers who were patiently waiting for
God to act on His promises.

In Week Three the theme is 'Songs of Joy'. Here we
will study songs such as Mary's *'Magnificat'* and Simeon's
'Nunc Dimitis'.

In Week Four the theme is 'Saviour of Joy', and through
readings from the 'prologue' to John's Gospel we will
consider the Person of Christ and the miracle of the
incarnation.

In Week Five the theme will be 'Gifts of Joy', focusing
on the latecomers to the cradle, the Wise Men, and we
will prepare for the celebration of Epiphany.

Let Advent joy begin!

World of Joy

Let us begin our Advent journey with the sober reminder that the Bible begins the story of salvation with the setting of a joyless world.

This is the message of the first eleven chapters of Genesis: A perfect world pronounced by the Maker as 'good', descends into a joyless, fractious world. Man and woman retreat from warm fellowship with the Creator to guilty hiding and eventual banishment from the garden of delight. Family life moves from the potential of harmonious partnership to murderous jealousy. A healthy creative approach to work soon degenerates into the arrogant building of a towering temple so the builders can 'make a name for themselves'.

This world urgently needs a message of joy!

And so God implements His plan of salvation, which begins with one man in Genesis 12 and will culminate with the world of nations residing in a renewed world of joy in Revelation 22.

Our Advent journey commences with the prophet Malachi, who reminds us of the need to guard our faith in a waiting period. Then we consider Abraham, and how God's promises to him are unfolded through descendants such as Ruth and David – all members of the family tree of Jesus (Matt. 1:1–17).

Waiting for Christmas

Bible passage
Malachi 3:1–5,16–18

I spend much of my time flying to and from London Heathrow. When the brochure for the new Terminal 5 was published, I was promised that British Airways' new home would transform my travel experience. I eagerly read the publicity on T5 and discovered the main departure area is the size of ten football pitches, the baggage system transports 12,000 bags per hour around the terminal, the water-harvesting scheme reuses up to eighty-five per cent of the rainfall that falls on Terminal 5's campus.

All very impressive, but I scanned the publicity in vain for one tiny piece of personal information. Would T5 tackle my problem of waiting? You see, my total time of waiting at Heathrow probably adds up to a few years of my life. I have got used to humming 'When peace like a river' when stuck in another queue. In many areas of discipleship I know I am growing, but I need bucket loads of grace to cope with a waiting period.

It is Advent. This is the waiting season when we are invited to look back and listen to the familiar readings from the Old Testament prophets who prophesied the coming of the Messiah. Isaiah prophesied there would be a Messiah from God who would be a Wonderful Counsellor, a Mighty God, an Everlasting Father and a Prince of Peace. And the people of God waited 800 years for this promise to be fulfilled.

During Advent we rejoice that in the fullness of time God did send His Son (Gal. 4:4), but Advent reminds us that we are still in a waiting period. We await the return of Christ the King, who is coming to judge the world in righteousness at the end of the age.

We wait in the tension between celebrating the arrival of the Servant King in the lowliness of the Bethlehem stable and anticipating the promised arrival of the King of Glory in His triumphal return. And the people of God have been waiting for the fulfilment of this promise for 2,000 years.

Waiting periods can be a challenge to faith.

Malachi has been called the prophet of the waiting period. His book is the last in the Old Testament and it is estimated that when he put down his pen centuries went by before the birth of Jesus. It was 400 years of waiting.

Malachi was raised up by God to strengthen faith in a waiting period, and his message is relevant for today. His message is: In a waiting period, guard your grand purpose (Mal. 1:11).

Pause for thought

God has a grand purpose for the world – to make His name great among the nations. Waiting for God to deliver on His promises can become a huge burden (1:13). Instead, be inspired by the beautiful picture in Malachi of how to wait. Faithful people gather together to share their hope in the promises of God. God records in writing their prayers and worship and fellowship (3:16). It is a lesson in how to wait.

Prayer for today

The Wonderful Counsellor guide you
The Mighty God protect you
The Everlasting Father be with you
The Prince of Peace overshadow you
And the blessing of God be upon you
Now and evermore
Amen

Reflection

A lady once came to Watchman Nee, the twentieth-century Chinese Christian author and church leader, and asked him to pray for her. She said, 'I need more patience in my life.'

Watchman Nee began to pray: 'Lord, this sister needs patience, so I pray you will bring into her life tribulations, difficulties and hardships.'

The woman stopped him and said, 'I asked you to pray for more patience.'

Watchman Nee said, 'But you don't understand. The Bible says tribulation works patience' (Rom. 5:3).

This answer sounds harsh, as we know that tribulation and suffering sometimes produce bitterness and anger. The point Watchman Nee was making, however, was that through tribulation we can discover that God is supporting us, and through this experience our faith in Him can grow.

2 Dec

Seeking a new beginning

Bible passage
Genesis 12:1–4

If you are shopping for board games this Christmas, you may be interested to discover there are over thirty different versions of Monopoly available for purchase online.

Anti-Monopoly is played between two teams. The 'Competitors' charge fair rents and can build on any street. The 'Monopolists' charge high rents and can only build on streets they own, but they can go to prison for price-fixing!

Bibliopoly combines the fun of a property trading game with remarkable cities of the Bible. Players start 'In the Beginning' and journey through Bible cities. It's all fun and games until someone lands on 'Go Meditate', and has to miss three turns!

For the more serious-minded, there is the British Museum. There you will find the Royal Game of Ur, one of the oldest board games in the world. The Royal Game of Ur was discovered during the 1920s when Sir Charles Leonard Woolley was excavating ancient Mesopotamian burial sites in the city of Basra, located in modern-day Iraq. Woolley and his team were able to piece together how the people of Ur lived and what they believed.

The port of Ur in ancient times was the gateway to the Middle East. Living in this community would give you an awareness of pagan worship including the bull worship of Crete, the animal gods of Egypt, the sun gods of Syria and the sensual deities of India.

It was in this world that God found a man called Abraham. We know very little about his family apart from the reference to his father, Terah, who 'worshipped other gods' (Josh. 24:2) and whose name is connected with the moon goddess who was worshipped at Ur. Abraham and his family would have learnt the religious mantras – light a candle and your sailors will be safe during the storms; burn some incense at the temple and your caravans will not be attacked; put some food out for the gods and your harvest will be bountiful.

However, in this world of pagan religions, Abraham was searching for a deeper meaning to life. We don't know how the Lord prepared the heart of this man living in this culture, but the Bible says God spoke and Abraham listened and obeyed Him (Gen. 12:1–4).

Pause for thought
As we begin our Advent journey, let's remember that we are surrounded by cultures which increasingly take Christ out of Christmas to make it a Xmas celebration. Are we too judgmental about these prevailing cultures? Can we dare to believe that people like Abraham are living in the streets of our community? They may be seeking the deeper meaning of life and a new beginning with God.

The story of Abraham reminds us that wherever men and women are seeking sincerely for the deeper meaning of life, God meets those who seek Him with all their heart (Jer. 29:13).

Prayer for today
    Advent God, we worship you: the God who comes.
    You are not remote from the world you have made,
    But each day you come to us,
    Blessing us with your presence.
    Grant us the grace to welcome your coming.
    Inflame our love to yearn for your presence.
    Enlarge our vision to recognise your coming day by day.
    We greet you, Advent God.[1]

Reflection
Think of those in your community who are seeking a new beginning with God. Pray for them.

3 Dec

Saying 'Yes' to God's promises

Bible passage
Genesis 12:4–5

Some of my friends are incredibly well prepared for the busy season of Christmas. In January they buy cut-price Christmas cards in the sales. In April they begin knitting for the grandchildren's gifts. In July they purchase thoughtful presents for their relatives. By the end of September they have prepared an updated Christmas card list. In October they are searching for online bargains on eBay. At the beginning of December their annual letter is one of the first through the letterbox. This is what I call a carefully managed and finely organised Christmas!

But be warned – God can be the divine disturber of the managed life.

Like most of our lives, Abraham's life was probably full of family routine – sleep, work, rest and play. But also like us, he carried burdens and sadness in his life. He and his ageing wife Sarah were childless and his youngest brother had died. In spite of these traumas, his family ties were close and in line with the customs of his day – Abraham stayed close to his father Terah. Then one day, after his father's death, God came knocking at Abraham's door.

God's message to Abraham was profound – it was all about blessing: God promises that He will bless Abraham; He promises that Abraham will be a blessing; He promises to bless those who bless Abraham. And the big promise – not to be missed – is that all the families of the earth will count themselves blessed through Abraham.

This collection of promises to Abraham set in motion a train of events that would eventually lead to the birth of Jesus in Bethlehem. Somehow we need to get our minds around the idea that Jesus

Himself was 'in the loins' of Abraham. This promise of blessing is so important that Paul says God was announcing the gospel in advance when He said to Abraham, 'All nations will be blessed through you' (Gal. 3:8).

The promise only became active when Abraham said 'Yes' to God's invitation. God's intention to bless the nations is combined with a human commitment to obedience. Only the leaving can release the blessing.

Pause for thought

The story of Abraham has been described as a 75-year-old man taking off his slippers and putting on his walking boots. He said 'Yes' to God's promises.

The virgin Mary's response to the angelic messenger was, 'I am the Lord's servant … May it be to me as you have said' (Luke 1:38). God only requires our 'Yes' in response to His promises.

Prayer for today

Lord, when You visit me with Your promises
Strengthen me so I am not afraid
May I not be so settled in my managed life
That I am unable to be free for Your higher purposes for me.
Help me to say 'Yes.'

Reflection

Mary is the ideal recipient of presents, it seems. She's the kind of person who accepts the gift with delighted curiosity and waits to see how it works …
How lovely of God to give the best gift, the gift of Jesus, to someone who knows how to accept presents cheerfully. Any present God is going to give is likely to have unforeseen consequences, and it may not be exactly what you had asked for, but it may also change your life in ways that you couldn't imagine or begin to hope for.[2]

4 Dec

Are you prepared to make a journey?

Bible passage
Genesis 12:6–9

Christmas is a busy time of year for travelling. It is the occasion when thousands of us make long journeys for family reunions. I remember one Christmas Eve we shoe-horned the family into our car for a four-hour journey to the West Country. On board was one mum and one dad, two children and one grandma, one golden retriever dog and one turkey (stuffed) and Christmas presents wrapped in the largest parcels imaginable. I was just grateful my relatives had not requested us to bring a Christmas tree!

It took military precision to plan the journey. We knew the time of departure and the stopping points on the route, we knew our destination and the plan of action when we arrived and, most importantly for our relatives, we knew the day and time of departure.

So, just imagine a journey of a lifetime with no fixed destination, no specific timetable and some very unpredictable outcomes.

God's promises to Abraham involved a journey which was breathtaking in its vision: '... all peoples on earth will be blessed through you' (Gen. 12:3). God's plan began with a man who was willing to make a journey based on a cluster of promises which would culminate in a blessing for the whole world. But note – the man who is promised the legacy of being the father of a vast nation does not even have a son to bear his name.

The journey of Abraham begins with major sacrifices. He is called by God to separate himself from the familiar and secure landmarks that have been a feature of his life. The sacrifice involves leaving his country, his culture and his family roots. The experience of Abraham is a reminder that major acts of renunciation lie at the heart of every great adventure with God (Luke 9:23–25).

If you want to find your life, get ready to lose your certainties. Losing your life may mean surviving without your fixed destinations, specific timetables and predictable outcomes.

Abraham was being led on a special journey, and the destination lay completely in God's hands. If you read the repetitive 'I wills' of verses 2 and 3 of Genesis 12, you will see the writer is emphasising that the greater part of this pilgrim's progress into the unknown is masterminded by God. Abraham's total dependence on God is symbolised by the altars he built and the prayers he offered (vv.7–8).

Pause for thought

When God plans to bring joy to the world, it frequently involves believers in a journey. We make the sacrificial journey of courageous faith and build our altars of prayer and trust. And we leave God to do the impossible (Luke 1:37).

Prayer for today

We arrange our lives as best we can,
   to keep your holiness at bay,
      with our pieties,
         our doctrines,
         our liturgies,
         our moralities,
         our secret ideologies,
Safe, virtuous, settled.
And then you –
  you and your dreams,
  you and your visions,
  you and your purposes,
  you and your commands,
  you and our neighbors.
We find your holiness not at bay,
  but probing, pervading,
    insisting, demanding.
And we yield, sometimes gladly,
   sometimes resentfully,
   sometimes late ... or soon.
We yield because you, beyond us, are our God.
We are your creatures met by your holiness,
   by your holiness made our true selves.
And we yield. Amen.[3]

5 Dec

When faith grinds to a halt

Bible passage
Ruth 1:1–13

My maternal grandmother lived near Consett, County Durham, and was an amazing woman who lived to six months short of her one-hundredth birthday. When she was in her nineties, suffering from another broken limb from which she would eventually recover, the local doctor reputedly told her, 'Mrs Willis, you are so healthy you will never die – we will have to shoot you!'

I loved spending holidays with my grandmother. She gave me permission to eat my pudding before my main meal and we were allowed to have fruitcake, rice pudding and jam tarts on the breakfast table (unheard of in my home). With her Irish farming background, my grandmother was full of stories and witticisms.

She conveyed spiritual truth with memorable aphorisms. Her standard phrase for an ethical dilemma was, 'What would Jesus do?' Her epigram for coping with the mystery of God's providence was, 'It will pass.' Her advice when circumstances were confusing was, 'Give God time.'

My grandmother knew and understood the main message behind the book of Ruth. Tucked away in the family tree of Jesus are Boaz and Ruth (Matt. 1:5), the parents of Obed, the grandfather of the great King David. Ruth and Boaz's story is a brilliant example of how God needs time to work out His loving purposes to bring joy to the world.

The book of Ruth opens with some joyless scenes of an unhappy family. Elimelech and his wife Naomi are residents in Bethlehem. When the harvest fails, Elimelech decides to move his wife and two sons to the neighbouring country of Moab, a nation with a reputation for pagan worship and child sacrifices.

Soon after the move to Moab, Elimelech dies and within ten years his two sons are also dead. As a widow, Naomi has the comfort and companionship of two devoted daughters-in-law, but her faith has been damaged by what she has suffered.

Naomi eventually makes her way back to her hometown of Bethlehem with one of her daughters-in-law, Ruth. She tells her old friends in Bethlehem that she is no longer called Naomi: 'Call me Mara, because the Almighty has made my life very bitter. I went away full, but the LORD has brought me back empty … The LORD has afflicted me; the Almighty has brought misfortune upon me' (Ruth 1:20–21).

Pause for thought
God's promise to Abraham involved a blessing to all the nations. With the sad story of Naomi there is a setback. It appears the promise is grinding to a halt and is about to sink into the sands of oblivion.

But when God's promises appear to be grinding to a halt, remember to give Him time. He needs time to work out His loving purposes. His loving purposes include the setbacks.

Prayer for today
Lord, Your way for me has always been clear
But today Your way is hidden
Help me to trust You when I cannot see You

Lord, Your word to me has always been plain
But today You seem to be silent
Help me to trust You when I cannot hear You

Lord, Your friendship to me has always been close
But today You seem far away
Help me to trust You when I feel friendless

Lord, Your promises to me have always been reliable
But today You seem to be absent
Help me to trust You when the ground is shifting

Lord, in spite of everything
Help me to give You time
I believe
Help my unbelief

Reflection

'For I know the plans I have for you,' declares the LORD, 'plans to prosper you and not to harm you, plans to give you hope and a future.'

Jeremiah 29:11

6 Dec

How to recover from the big mistakes

Bible passage
Ruth 1:14–18; 4:13–14

Ruth is one my favourite Bible characters. Her mother-in-law believes God has turned his back on the family, but Ruth sees enough of Naomi's faith to exclaim, *'I want your God to be my God'* (1:16).

Ruth moves to Bethlehem with her mother-in-law and they live on the borderline of poverty. She is employed by a landowner and falls in love with her employer Boaz. They are eventually married according to the ancient traditions of Bethlehem.

The marriage of Ruth and Boaz becomes a silent witness to the work of Jesus Christ in that both Boaz and Jesus are called kinsman-redeemers. In ancient family law, a kinsman-redeemer was someone who took a loving, costly initiative to secure the total redemption of a helpless person. The actions of Boaz towards Ruth mirror the relationship between Jesus and us. Jesus, our Redeemer, redeems the life of the believer at great cost.

Ruth gives birth to a baby boy and calls him Obed, which makes her the great grandmother of King David. Ruth has a central place in the family tree of Jesus (Matt. 1:5).

The family live happily ever after – especially proud Grandma Naomi! The good wishes of the women of Bethlehem ring in her ears: 'May he [your grandson] become famous throughout Israel!' (Ruth 4:14). God's promise lives on!

Pause for thought

God works out His loving purposes in the everyday lives of
ordinary people
In the mistakes we make in decision-making
In bereavement and sadness
In family love and committed relationships
In unemployment and work
In romance and marriage
In the birth of children
In the joy of grandchildren
In the fellowship of believers
In trusting God

Prayer for today

Lord, may Your kingdom come
Your will be done
On earth as it is in heaven

In the ordinary things of life
In the grinding routines
In the disciplined duties
In the thankless tasks

Lord, open my eyes to see where You are working in Your world
Help me to see Your footprints
And in them plant my own

Lord, may Your kingdom come
Your will be done
On earth as it is in heaven
Amen

Reflection

An older Christian gave me some advice when I was starting out as a
disciple of Jesus. He said I needed to know the way back as well as
the way in. The journey of the Christian life involves setbacks, and
when we have lost our way we need the challenging words of
Psalm 51. The opening verse of this psalm reminds us that we begin

on the way back by knowing we belong. For all the wretchedness David felt over the big mistake of his life, he knew he belonged to a God of unfailing love and great compassion. He presented himself as an undeserving candidate for the undeserved grace of God. Remember, Jesus is never shocked by our sin – in His grace He is drawn towards the sinner.

7 Dec

Trust God to make the right choice

Bible passages
2 Samuel 7:11–13,16; Luke 1:32–33

David has an important place in the family tree of the Messiah, which is why Jesus is so often referred to as 'the Son of David'. The Early Church noted his significant contribution to the story of salvation and in one of his sermons, Paul reminds his congregation that David was a man after God's own heart. The reason for this affectionate title was that David did everything God wanted him to do (Acts 13:22).

The reason for this family link between David and Jesus is clearly seen in our Old Testament passage for today. God anointed David to be the leader of the nation. This blessing on David's life was to be imparted to his descendants. However, in spite of the possibility of human failure, there was always an eternal element to God's choice of David. God was planning for a definitive single ruler who would rule a kingdom that would never come to an end. In making His promise of an everlasting kingdom, God had in mind 'great David's greater son' Jesus Christ (2 Sam. 7:16).

The promise of an eternal kingdom was included by the Angel Gabriel in his announcement to the mother of Jesus. Mary's baby Son would be the King of the kingdom that will never end (Luke 1:32–33).

In the opening chapters of his Gospel, Luke puts great emphasis on the ancestral links between Jesus and David. The house of David is mentioned (1:69); he identifies Bethlehem as the town of David (2:4); the family tree includes David (3:31). The message of the

Bible is plain – the stories of David and Jesus are closely connected. But what an amazing choice God made when David was anointed as king! David is the only person in the Bible described as 'a man after God's own heart'. He is the poet–musician who composes exquisite psalms. He is the successful warrior king who has been the inspiration of military commanders. He is the politician–diplomat who can bind a disparate group of tribal chiefs into a united nation. He is the visionary who is prepared to put God first when it comes to plans for temple building.

But there is an another side to this complex character. There is devious David; brutal David; angry David; adulterous David; David the murderer; David the failed parent.

Eugene Peterson describes the story of David as 'a plunge into the earthiness of our humanity'. If you want a biblical example of a man behaving badly, David is that person.

Pause for thought

So why did God choose David? For the same reason He chooses us. Out of His great love for us, even with all our imperfections and failures. God chooses us with the loving purpose of transforming us into men and women of whom He can say, 'They are people after my own heart.'

Prayer for today

Create in me a clean heart, O God,
and put a new and right spirit within me.
Do not cast me away from your presence,
and do not take your holy spirit from me.
Restore to me the joy of your salvation,
and sustain in me a willing spirit.

Then I will teach transgressors your ways,
and sinners will return to you ...

O Lord, open my lips,
and my mouth will declare your praise.

Psalm 51:10–13,15, NRSV

Reflection

As an instance of humanity in himself, he isn't much. He has little wisdom to pass on to us on how to live successfully. He was an unfortunate parent and an unfaithful husband. From a purely historical point of view he was a barbaric chieftain with a talent for poetry. But David's importance isn't in his morality or his military prowess but in his experience and witness to God. Every event in his life was a confrontation with God.[4]

Suggestion for group activity – Week One

The Jesse Tree

The suggestion for group activity this week is to create a Jesse Tree. A Jesse Tree is a tree branch decorated with symbols representing the stories of people in Jesus' family tree. In Isaiah 11:1 we read, 'A shoot will come up from the stump of Jesse; from his roots a Branch will bear fruit.' Jesse was the father of David, Israel's greatest king, and it was from David's lineage that Jesus came.

During Advent it is good to remember some of the people who came before Jesus and who were waiting and hoping for the birth of the Messiah. Each day from 1 to 25 December, we can hang a symbol on the Jesse Tree to remember those people who were part of Jesus' family.

Here are some suggestions for incorporating the Jesse Tree in your celebrations. The resources at the end of this section offer further inspiration.

1. Plan ahead in your Advent programme and arrange an all-age family tea on the first Sunday of Advent. Teach the meaning of the Jesse Tree and then demonstrate how to make one with the accompanying ornaments and an appropriate Bible verse for each day.

2. In your mid-week house group, make a Jesse Tree in the form of a banner or poster for a wall, with the symbols fastened to it. A banner can be as plain or as elaborate as your imagination dictates. Usually, a banner and symbols for a sanctuary are made of heavy felt, cotton or other appropriate fabric. The design is

embroidered onto the fabric and the symbols attached with pins or Velcro. One for the home or Sunday school classroom can be made from poster board, the design done with markers and coloured symbols, made from construction paper or cut from Christmas cards.

3. A variation on (2) is to have a ready-made Jesse Tree in the centre of the room. Prepare small cards with the names of Old Testament characters/Bible stories on them, and attach ribbon or wool to each to enable the cards to be hung on the branches of the Jesse Tree. Encourage your house group members to either look up and read the Bible passages or, better still, to spontaneously tell the story of the Bible character on their card. For example: 'Hello, my name is Abraham. My life was basic and routine until one day God spoke to me and life was never the same again ...', and so on. Set a time limit on how long each storyteller speaks for!

As an introduction to these group activities, explain that the purpose of the Jesse Tree is to tell the story of God in the Old Testament and to connect the Advent season with the faithfulness of God throughout 4,000 years of history.

Resources
Geraldine McCaughrean's *The Jesse Tree* with illustrations by Bee Willey (Oxford: Lion Hudson, 2003). A brilliant award-winning book.
The following sites include creative ideas for using Jesse Trees: www.rca.org; www.shalfleet.net; www.jesse-tree.com

1. Christopher J. Ellis and Myra Blyth for the Baptist Union of Great Britain *Gathering for Worship: Patterns and Prayers for the Community of Disciples* (Norwich: Canterbury Press, 2005) p.351. Used by permission.
2. Jane Williams *Approaching Christmas* (Oxford: Lion Hudson, 2005) p.58.
3. From *Awed to Heaven, Rooted in Earth* by Walter Brueggemann, copyright © 2002 Fortress Press. Used by permission of Augsburg Fortress Publishers.
4. Eugene Peterson, *Leap Over a Wall: Earthy Spirituality for Everyday Christians* (New York: HarperCollins, 1997) p.5.

WEEK TWO
Community of Joy

Advent is a reminder of what it means to wait patiently for something that God has promised. This week's readings focus on a community of believers who were waiting for the promised Messiah. As one Bible version translates it, 'The people were on the tiptoe of expectation ...' (Luke 3:15, NEB).

The unexpected element in each of the stories is that these people on tiptoe did not expect to have such a personal involvement in the fulfilment of God's plans. They were probably immersed in their daily routine, but were spiritually disciplined enough to recognise the signs that God was at work in a special way.

The elderly couple Elizabeth and Zechariah have prayed for a child for many years. The engaged couple Mary and Joseph are planning their wedding. The faithful intercessors Simeon and Anna are yearning for the arrival of the Messiah. The nightshift shepherds are working on the farm when the choir of angels burst in with the breaking news that a special baby has been born in nearby Bethlehem.

We need to be 'on the tiptoe of expectation' as God speaks to us this week.

The elderly couple

Bible passage
Luke 1:5–7

People are placed in a dilemma when waiting for a bus that is late: do they start to walk or do they continue to wait? It all depends on your psyche. Those who are patient at waiting read a book, complete a crossword or compile a list. The impatient start to walk!

We spend our lives waiting – waiting for Christmas, waiting for the end of the working day, waiting for a relative to die, waiting for the violence to end, waiting for the test results, waiting for a child to be born. Luke keeps us waiting as he commences his amazing story about Jesus. His first chapter is eighty verses of long waiting, and still Jesus has not been born. While Luke keeps us waiting for the birth of Jesus, he tells us the story of an elderly couple who had been waiting a lifetime for a baby.

Luke wants us to see history repeating itself. The elderly childless couple reminds us of the experience of Abraham and Sarah (Gen. 16:1–2); the visit of the angelic messenger and the speechlessness of Zechariah (1:18) are similar to the experience of Daniel (Dan. 10:1–17); the words of prophecy to Zechariah (1:17) are a direct fulfilment of the closing words of the prophet Malachi (Mal. 4:5–6).

Both Elizabeth and Zechariah belonged to the famous priestly dynasty of Aaron. This gave Zechariah the right to take his place among the estimated 18,000 priests who were entitled to serve in the Jerusalem temple. The fact that Elizabeth was part of the prestigious ancestry of Aaron was like the daughter of a bishop marrying a vicar!

Their childlessness was a great burden to them, especially to Elizabeth (1:25). To counter suggestions that their childlessness was a sign of God's judgment on some hidden sin in their lives (a common belief in those days – Lev. 20:21; Jer. 22:30), Luke says these are two godly people. Their names have meaning. Zechariah means 'Yahweh has remembered again' and Elizabeth can be interpreted 'My God is the one by whom I swear'. Their characters are 'upright and blameless'. This does not imply they were sinless, but it is a description of two people who were vigilant in obeying the laws of God and faithful in attending the Temple services.

The community had wrongly interpreted their childlessness as a reproach from God but in fact they were about to be candidates for God's blessing. They belonged to that community of godly people who had prayed and waited, and their faith was eventually rewarded. This is a reminder of the births of Isaac (Gen. 18:11), Samson (Judg. 13:2,5) and Samuel (1 Sam. 1–2).

Pause for thought

God always intended that His people would be the community through whom He would demonstrate His love to the world (Gen. 12:1–3).

There had been centuries of waiting for the promised Messiah.

While we wait, God is working. In His time He fulfils His promises.

Prayer for today

Let me depend on God alone:
who never changes,
who knows what is best for me
so much better than I;
and gives in a thousand ways, at all times,
All that the perfect Father can
for the child's good growth –
things needful, things salutary,
things wise, beneficent and happy.

Thy gifts and will are one:
it is thy being to will and give what is best:
for thy will issues from thy love;
the more I do thy will, the more I learn thy love;
and the more I learn thy love, the more I am impelled

to do thy whole will.
So, Father, thy will be sought, be found,
be followed, loved and finished.[1]

Reflection

Tom Wright suggests that the Eucharist is the anticipation of the
future when heaven and earth are made new: 'It is the breaking
in of God's future, the Advent future, into our present time.
Every Eucharist is a little Christmas as well as a little Easter.'[2]

9 Dec

The doubting pastor

Bible passage
Luke 1:18,25

When Philip Yancey turned fifty, he had a complete physical check-
up. At the same time he scheduled a spiritual check-up and went on
a silent retreat. During days of solitude, he pondered what changes
he needed to make to keep his soul in shape. The more he listened
to God, the longer grew the list of his spiritual action plan. Top of
his list was to question his doubts as much as his faith. He says, 'I
brood on doubts and experience faith in occasional flashes. Isn't it
about time for me to reverse the pattern?'[3]

The verses today are a contrast between doubt and belief in the
same family. Zechariah had left the hillside home and made his
way to Jerusalem to serve in the Temple. He was one of the 18,000
priests who were organised into twenty-four divisions. Each division
had the responsibility of one week of duties twice a year. There
were further divisions of family rotas that drew lots to decide who
would enter the Holy Place, burn the incense and offer the whole
burnt offering.

It may be a challenge to faith to realise that the random falling of
a lot is a prelude to the turning-point in the life of this family.

The Holy Place was where incense was burned at sunrise and

dusk. What the priest did served as a symbol of the intercessions of the people in the outer courts of the Temple. We don't know the exact content of Zechariah's prayers in the Holy Place, but when the angelic messenger suddenly appeared to him, the reassuring words of the angel were: 'Do not be afraid ... your prayer has been heard' (Luke 1:13). Zechariah was a man in shock, He was 'gripped with fear' (v.12) – taken aback and deeply anxious.

The message to Zechariah was specific. Your wife is going to give birth to a son; his name has already been chosen – you will call him John; he will be a joy to you and to the community; he will have a distinctive lifestyle; his ministry will be spirit-filled and fruitful (vv.13–17)

Zechariah finds this message of good news unbelievable. Pious pastor he may be, however, his best response to the startling news is to exclaim, *But my wife and I are senior citizens!'* (v.18). His default position reveals the weakness of wanting firm evidence (1 Cor. 1.22), 'The certainty which leaves no room for doubt and incidentally no room for faith.'[4]

The pastor whose ministry is to bring people nearer to God is struggling to believe that God has responded to his prayers. Because of his unguarded words he is struck dumb until the day his son is born. In his silent world he reflects on how God has been working in his life, and out of this tomb of solitude will emerge a spirit-filled song of thanksgiving (Luke 1:67–79).

Pause for thought

The most spiritually-minded people can be overtaken with doubts. Is there a prayer you have been waiting for God to answer? How will you respond when the answer comes?

Prayer for today

Lord, in this season of noise and bustle
Silence me

Create some sacred space in my life
Address me

Challenge me with the impossible
Startle me

Remind me of Your promises
Settle me

Give me time to reflect on Your goodness
Hide me

Prepare me for joyful events
Train me

Arouse in me a spirit of thanksgiving and praise
Inspire me

I am now ready to serve You today
Send me

Reflection

This story is about much more than Zechariah's joy at having
a son at last, or Elisabeth's exultation in being freed from
the scorn of the mothers in the village. It is about the great
fulfilment of God's promises and purposes. But the needs,
hopes and fears of ordinary people are not forgotten in this
larger story, precisely because of who Israel's God is – the God
of lavish, self giving love, as Luke will tell us in so many ways
throughout his gospel.[5]

10 Dec

The young teenager

Bible passage

Luke 1:26–37

It was the Oxford newspaper headline that grabbed my attention:
'Million pound paintings found in spare bedroom'.

The story behind the headline involved the death of an elderly
academic called Jean Preston. In the 1960s she had bought two
paintings for £200. The paintings, from the fifteenth century, depicted

two saints and were part of an eight-piece altar panel; six of the panels had been found, but the location of the missing two panels was one of the art world's unsolved mysteries.

After Jean Preston's death in 2006, an art history expert found the panels behind the door of the spare bedroom in Jean's Oxford house. The two paintings were subsequently sold at auction for an estimated £1.7 million, and the auctioneer was quoted as saying: 'To put it in a nutshell, we are dealing with two works of art painted by one of the greats, it simply does not get much better than that.'

And the artist's name? It was Fra Angelico.

The name Fra Angelico is etched in my memory. A few years ago my wife and I enjoyed a summer holiday in Italy and we visited Florence. We were encouraged by a knowledgeable friend to avoid the crowds thronging to see Michelangelo's celebrated statue of David and instead visit San Marco, and in the tranquillity of that ancient monastery to view the breathtaking beauty of the devotional frescoes by Fra Angelico.

His fresco of the annunciation is exquisite. The artist had captured brilliantly the visit of the Angel Gabriel to the Virgin Mary. There is a hesitation in the folded arms of the angel as he delivers the weighty message from God; there is a submission in the folded arms of Mary as she listens obediently to God's Word. This visitation will change Mary's life and the course of world history forever.

Sit somewhere quiet and read aloud the Bible passage for today, then think carefully about Mary.

Mary is a virgin with no sexual experience. In everything but sexual intimacy, Mary and Joseph are 'married', and Joseph refers to Mary as his wife. After one year of engagement the marriage will be consummated.

The news that Mary will become pregnant, without her knowing Joseph sexually, is deeply troubling for the young woman. Mary's question to the angel is not doubt or fear, but a simple request for clarification: 'How will this be … since I am a virgin?' (v.34).

The answer is the overshadowing power of God (v.35). The Creator God will breathe by His Holy Spirit into the body of Mary and she will conceive a child; the protecting presence of God which is likened to a mighty eagle will overshadow the life of Mary and her unborn child (Psa. 91:4).

Nothing is impossible with God (Luke 1:37).

Pause for thought

Mary is the model disciple. She gave God her 'Yes' in spite of the cost involved. Her advice to other disciples is, 'Do whatever he [Jesus] tells you' (John 2:5).

Prayer for today

Lord, You can do with me as You wish
In Your time
In Your way
For I am Your willing servant
Today
Always
Overshadow me with Your presence
Amen

Reflection

Mary is not singled out because she was immaculately conceived or perpetually virginal. In a very full sense she was simply a *woman*, and as a woman was as significant as all women are in God's eyes and in God's dealings with the world.[6]

11 Dec

The loving cousins

Bible passage
Luke 1:39–45

My grandson said to my wife recently, 'What was it like in the black and white days, Grandma?' He had probably heard some reference to the older members of our family watching the 1953 Coronation on a television set showing black and white pictures. His phrase was a polite catchword for anything that for him was B.E. – before emails.

So, in the B.E. age, can we imagine what was it like for someone in Bible times who was bursting to share some good news with a close relative? In Mary's case it meant walking a distance of nearly

100 miles, a journey of three or four days, to visit her cousin Elizabeth.

Here are two expectant mothers. One considered too old to conceive. One almost too young to be a mother. Both surprised by God. Both strengthened by the companionship of the other. Both expressing an obedient willingness to be the servants of the Lord. *Nothing is impossible with God.*

This is the story of two pregnant women, relating because of the work of the Holy Spirit in their lives. Their experience anticipates the work of the Holy Spirit on the Day of Pentecost. Elizabeth is filled with the Holy Spirit and prophesies with a loud voice. Mary is filled with the song of the Holy Spirit as she magnifies God her Saviour. These works of the Holy Spirit are not revealed through a high priest or a chief rabbi, but prayerful believing women in a hillside village are the first to celebrate the Christ-child. *Nothing is impossible with God.*

This is the occasion when a baby danced before it was born. Before John points to Jesus as the Lamb of God (John 1:29), he leaps in the womb to share the good news of the identity of the baby Mary carries. In thirty years' time John will be preaching, 'Prepare the way for the Lord, make straight paths for him' (Mark 1:3). *Nothing is impossible with God.*

Here is an opportunity to celebrate down-to-earth caring friendship. The teenager and the senior citizen, sharing, caring and rejoicing together. Shared joy in the Holy Spirit and caring friendship breaks down all the barriers. *Nothing is impossible with God.*

Pause for thought

Can we imagine our meetings for friendship becoming encounters with God? How would Elizabeth and Mary understand that our bodies are temples of the Holy Spirit (1 Cor. 3:16)? How should we appreciate this truth?

Prayer for today

Gracious God
Who gave joy to Elizabeth and Mary as they recognised
The signs of redemption at work within them
Help us to know the work of the Lord deep within us

May His joy spill out of lives
That the world may also rejoice in Your salvation
Through Jesus Christ our Lord
Amen

Reflection

While he was saying these things, some woman lifted her voice
above the murmur of the crowd: 'Blessed the womb that carried
you, and the breasts at which you nursed!'
Jesus commented, 'Even more blessed are those who hear God's
Word and guard it with their lives!'

Luke 11:27–28, The Message

12 Dec

The anxious fiancé

Bible passage

Matthew 1:18–25

I have attended many school Nativity plays and I think it is the
unpredictability of these occasions that makes them memorable.
When children depart from the set script it can be the highlight of
the evening.

One of my highlights was when Joseph appealed poignantly for a
room in the inn, asking the innkeeper to have some pity for Mary's
condition. The innkeeper responded hardheartedly by saying, 'Her
condition is nothing to do with me,' to which Joseph responded
swiftly, 'But it's nothing to do with me either!'

This is how Matthew introduces us to Joseph. He is the man
who has nothing to do with the conception of the child in Mary's
womb. He is betrothed to Mary, which means in Jewish law they are
referred to as husband and wife but are not yet living under one roof
and sharing the marriage bed.

We must assume the young carpenter was a normal man with
healthy appetites. There would be shared secrets, joyful planning
and carefree laughter between the young couple. Then one day

his dream crashes into the worst imaginable nightmare. To repeat Matthew's words: '... she was found to be with child through the Holy Spirit' (v.18).

Imagine Joseph's reaction when Mary breaks the news that she is pregnant. Joseph knows he has not slept with Mary; she claims she has not been unfaithful – yet she is pregnant and a virgin.

Joseph is now a man in pain and confusion. Mary's story was so unbelievable it strained to the limits of his faith and his love. But wisdom prevails and the godly character of Joseph shines through. He decides to divorce Mary quietly (Deut. 24:1). Alexander Maclaren terms this as 'the last gift his wounded soul could give her'.[7]

Then the man with shattered dreams is given a real dream. The clear message of the angels is that God is in charge of this unbelievable event and we are witnessing the fulfilment of God's promise in Scripture (Matt. 1:22–23; Isa. 7:14).

What a difference a dream makes! When Joseph awoke he did exactly as the angel had commanded. He gave the unborn child a name and eventually a home. This action of Joseph bestowed on Jesus the legal status of being the Son of David.

Pause for thought
By his obedience, Joseph is another prototype disciple for us to consider. His life only finds meaning in the Person of Jesus. His life is overshadowed by the actions of Jesus. Because of his relationship to Jesus he experiences the cost of discipleship. Who can estimate the snide ridicule he and Mary endured from sections of the community because of the unusual pregnancy?

Prayer for today
Lord, when our dreams turn into nightmares
Help us to stay calm
Jesus – come and rescue us from our sins
Immanuel – be with us in this time of desolation
Speak to us in our dreams
Show us how we can trust again those whom we love
Give us courage to follow where You are leading
Give us grace to cope with the stigmas of discipleship
We open the door of our house to Your gentle knock

Come, Lord Jesus
Fellowship with us in this home

Reflection

His [Joseph's] contribution to the physical outworking of the incarnation was indispensable, yet he never said a word that was recorded. He is a very strong reminder of the fact that God has a need of people just to care for and take care of others if their work for God is to be done.[8]

13 Dec

The prayer warrior

Bible passage
Luke 2:25–35

Lionel Blue says he obtained spiritual enlightenment while riding on the London Underground. One night he was listening to two young people who were sitting opposite him on the train.

'I love you,' the young man said to his girlfriend.

'And I love you even more,' was the warm response.

'But I love you even more than that,' replied the young man.

Then Lionel Blue said he realised the baby talk of the young lovers explained a spiritual problem he had never really understood before. He says, 'I was annoyed at that time by the worn out repetitions of our liturgy. Surely once was enough. Then I realised that liturgy was the language of love. If you were in love, you could repeatedly say the words and they would never seem banal. But if you weren't in love with God, love language seemed tiresome and repetitive.'[9]

Luke says that Simeon was a righteous and devout believer (v.25). Out of his deep love for God, Simeon repeated some worn out repetitions in the liturgy of the synagogue and the Temple. The prophet Zephaniah gave a perfect description of faithful worshippers like Simeon when he said there would be a remnant of meek and humble people who trusted in the name of the Lord. These people would 'do no wrong; they will speak no lies, nor will deceit be found in their mouths' (Zeph. 3:12–13).

Simeon built his life on a godly character. The habits of the heart brought him to worship, where he would memorise the Psalms and hear expositions of the Law and the Prophets. This piety shaped the mind of Simeon so he was looking to see where God was at work in the world. The phrase 'waiting for the consolation of Israel' (v.25) was a standard formulae referring to those who were longing for the arrival of the promised Messiah.

Simeon never ceased to hope that God would fulfil all His promises. We know that in the context of his prayer life, God had given him a specific promise. It had been revealed to Simeon by the Holy Spirit that he would not die before he had seen the promised Messiah (Luke 2:26).

Simeon was wide open to the influential work of the Holy Spirit for larger issues of life. In three successive verses we learn that the Holy Spirit was upon him, that the Holy Spirit revealed things to him and that the Holy Spirit moved him in timing his visits to the Temple (vv.25–27). This is a believer, who trained himself to be spiritually sensitive to the promptings of the Lord, so when the greatest day in his life arrives he is ready and prepared. When Simeon meets Mary and Joseph and baby Jesus he has a heart and mind ready to bless this family. Then Simeon said his personal prayer of thanksgiving: *Lord, I can now die a happy man because You have answered the prayers of a lifetime.*

Pause for thought

Simeon is a visual aid of the gospel: 'He took Jesus in his arms' (Luke 2:28). The Holy Spirit enabled him to recognise Jesus, welcome Jesus and receive Jesus. He confessed that all his prayers were answered because of Jesus.

Prayer for today

O Lord our God,
make us watchful and keep us faithful
as we await the coming of your Son our Lord;
that, when he shall appear,
he may not find us sleeping in sin

but active in his service
and joyful in his praise:
through Jesus Christ our Lord.[10]

14 Dec

The nightshift workers

Bible passage
Luke 2:8–20

What was that phrase in the Magnificat of Mary: 'He has brought down rulers from their thrones but has lifted up the humble' (Luke 1:52)? Here is the outworking of Mary's song in the events of the day. When God issues His edict that will be good news for the entire world, He bypasses the power of the emperor and chooses instead the poverty of the shepherds. The breaking news comes to the farm before it emerges in the palace.

The shepherds working in the fields belonged to the lowest paid of the working class. To supplement their income they hired themselves out as an agricultural Securicor, guarding sheep at night-times from marauding bandits and wild animals. The conservative religious despised shepherds because they neglected their religious duties. But in biblical history shepherds had an illustrious tradition. When Samuel went searching for a new king, he found God's anointed in the sheep fields (1 Sam. 16:10–13). Samuel knew that God's way of working reverses our human propensity to be impressed with outer splendour; He gives a higher place to the inner disposition of people (1 Sam. 16:7).

Choral music accompanied the first days of creation – Job describes it: '... morning stars sang together and all the angels shouted for joy ...' (Job 38:7). When God decides to send Jesus to earth, the beginning of the new creation is announced with another choral masterpiece. The angelic choir terrifies those working on the night shift with the message of joy to the world 'that will be for all the people'. Joy is such an appropriate harmony for Luke, and the melody lingers on through his writings: the joyful return of the disciples from a fruitful preaching mission (10:17); the joy of Jesus when the disciples grasp the revelation of the Father (10:21); the joy of a farmer who finds his lost sheep (15:5) (and see also 19:37; 24:41; 24:52; Acts 8:8; 16:34).

Are you humming this melody of joy?!

This joy-filled oratorio centres its message on the titles mentioned in Isaiah 9:1–7. The baby's name had been revealed to Mary and Joseph. The baby's identity was revealed to the shepherds. In David's city, Bethlehem, Someone special has been born. He is the Saviour, the Everlasting Father who will deliver His people and the Wonderful Counsellor who will comfort His people. He is the Christ, the anointed Messiah who will rule as a Prince of Peace and carry the government on His shoulders. He is the Lord, the Mighty God with sovereign authority over the entire cosmos.

As the story of the Saviour who is Christ the Lord unfolds in the preaching of the apostles, the implication of these magnificent titles becomes clear (Acts 2:33–36).

The only sign the shepherds are promised by the angel is a baby in an animal feeding trough, wrapped in strips of cloth to keep his tiny limbs protected. This is the Lord of Glory 'making himself nothing, taking the very nature of a servant, being made in human likeness' (Phil. 2:7).

Pause for thought

The first evangelists are a group of shepherds and an elderly widow in her eighties. The shepherds spread the word (Luke 2:17). Anna spoke about the child (v.38). These people were not called to be gifted preachers like Peter, learned Bible teachers like Paul or visionary writers like John. The shepherds and the elderly Anna simply shared what they had heard and seen. Sharing is the hallmark of those who belong to the Community of Joy (Acts 4:20; 1 John 1:3).

Prayer for today

Lord, I pray for the marginalised of this community
You share Your breaking news with unlikely people
The nightshift men and the elderly widows
The invisible people
The unimportant people

The forgotten people
Bring to my mind the faces of people I know
[Pause]
Save me from judging by outward appearances
Help me to read the true heart of people
Play that melody of joy to me once again
And make me a sharer of good news too

Reflection
The stable is bare, but the glory of God floods the story.[11]

Suggestion for group activity – Week Two

Christmas around the world
Plan this week to celebrate Christmas around the world. There are plenty of websites which can provide ideas, showing how different countries celebrate Advent.

Prepare some food snacks to represent the diversity of global cuisines. Play some world music to set the atmosphere.

Your church probably has links to missionaries or specific partnerships with local churches in various parts of the world. Why not link up with some of these friends and plan a Skype or telephone call during the meeting.

This meeting is a great opportunity to focus on the Persecuted Church. Many believers and their families will be living in fear during this season of Advent. Prepare for a time of prayer for your persecuted brothers and sisters in Christ. The following websites provide up-to-date information which you could draw on as a focus for your time of prayer: www.releaseinternational.org; www.csw.org.uk; www.persecution.com

If you want to focus on Bethlehem, plan well ahead and visit the Cave Gift Shop, Bethlehem, or their website www.annadwa.org. Go to the glassware section on this site where you can order tiny glass angels which can be used by your group as a symbol of solidarity with the world Church. There are other glassware items which are appropriate to Christmas.

There is a moving story about the making of these glass angels which is found on pages 135–141 of the book *Bethlehem Besieged: Stories of Hope in Times of Trouble* by Mitri Raheb (Minneapolis: Augsburg Fortress, 2004). Read this story at the end of the meeting. The glass angels tell the story of how God turns brokenness into beauty.

1. Eric Milner White, extract from 'Dependence', *My God, My Glory*, (London: SPCK, 1967) p.173. Used by permission.

2. N.T. Wright, *Surprised by Hope: Rethinking Heaven, the Resurrection, and the Mission of the Church* (HarperCollins, 2008) p.288.

3. Philip Yancey, 'A Believer's To-be List', *Christianity Today* magazine (March 2000).

4. G.B. Caird, *Saint Luke* (Pelican/Penguin Books, 1963) p.51.

5. Tom Wright, *Luke for Everyone* (London: SPCK, 2001) p.8.

6. Elaine Storkey quoted in David F. Wright (ed.), *Chosen by God – Mary in Evangelical Perspective* (London: Marshall, Morgan and Scott, 1989) p.196.

7. Alexander Maclaren, *The Gospel According to St. Matthew, Expositions of Holy Scripture* series (London: Hodder & Stoughton, 1905) p.8.

8. Tom Houston, *Characters around the Cradle* (Tain: Christian Focus Publications, 2002) p.74.

9. Lionel Blue, 'In the departure lounge of an airport', *The Tablet* (Market Harborough: The Tablet Publishing Company, December 2005).

10. Christopher J. Ellis and Myra Blyth for the Baptist Union of Great Britain *Gathering for Worship: Patterns and Prayers for the Community of Disciples* (Norwich: Canterbury Press, 2005) p.352. Used by permission.

11. Fred B. Craddock, *Luke, Interpretation Bible Commentaries* series (Louisville: John Knox Press, 1990) p.36.

WEEK THREE
Songs of Joy

Luke must have had a good ear for music. He knew that people learnt and remembered truth through song. Perhaps this is why he included four memorable songs of joy in his Christmas story.

In some traditions, three of Luke's songs are used in daily worship. Their respective titles are the first word or phrase of the songs from the Latin translation of the Bible: the *Benedictus* (Luke 1:68–79) is used in Morning Prayer; the *Magnificat* (Luke 1:46–55) is used in Evening Prayer; the *Nunc Dimitis* (Luke 2:29–32) at *Compline*, the final prayers of the day; and the *Gloria* (Luke 2:14) lies at the heart of many of our carols.

We will consider all these songs this week, as well as Hannah's song – which was probably a great influence on Mary and her own reflections in the *Magnificat* – the 'Song of Paul' from Philippians and the 'Songs of Supremacy' from Colossians.

God the Rock

Bible passage
1 Samuel 2:1–11

A friend of mine was driving through Brighton when he spotted a sign at the entrance to a building site. The strapline that grabbed his attention: 'Excuse us while we remove yesterday and make way for tomorrow.'

This may be a clever strapline for the building industry, but it cannot be applied if you want to understand the Christmas message. The Christmas strapline is: *'Excuse us while we focus on yesterday to make sense of today and tomorrow.'*

It was in the Scriptures of 'yesterday' that the main characters of the Nativity story found the meaning and purpose for what was happening in their lives. Mary was probably influenced by Hannah's song and used it to form some of her own reflections in the *Magnificat* (Luke 1:46–55).

The opening verses of 1 Samuel plunge us into a family conflict of painful proportions. Hannah was involved in a polygamous marriage which was the cause of great family misery. She was unable to conceive, and this brought about tension between her and the other woman in the marriage. Childlessness also carried the stigma of disgrace, as barrenness was considered a sign of divine judgment.

One day Hannah pours her soul out to God in the temple. In tears she pleads with Him for a child. She makes a solemn vow to the Lord that if He gives her a son, she will dedicate him to God's service. Eli the priest acts with great insensitivity towards Hannah, but eventually grasps what is happening. He gives her a blessing and Hannah leaves the place of worship in peace. In time the Lord blesses Hannah with her firstborn son, Samuel. The fruitfulness of answered prayer is shown in the fact that Hannah eventually becomes mother to three more sons and two daughters (1 Sam. 2:21)!

Hannah's life story probably blessed Mary in the following ways: She identified with the way Hannah felt helpless in her circumstances but was able to find her strength and security in God the rock (v.2). She identified with Hannah in her humiliation. For Hannah, it was the humiliation of barrenness; for Mary, the unforeseen pregnancy not understood by the wider community (v.1). Mary identified with Hannah in praising God for His concern for marginalised people: 'He raises the poor from the dust and lifts the needy from the ash heap ...' (v.8). Mary identified with Hannah in seeing that her blessing would be of great significance for the wider community of Israel (v.10).

Pause for thought
Hannah teaches us that we can be empowered by God to rise above a domestic crisis, however painful, to see His larger purpose being unfolded in our lives. God does have plans to prosper us and not to harm us (Jer. 29:11).

Prayer for today
Thank You, Lord, that things that are impossible with us
Become possible with You.
Let me see the values of Your upside-down kingdom
In my life today
Amen

Reflection
'For nothing is impossible with God.'

Luke 1:37

16 Dec

The *Magnificat*

Bible passage
Luke 1:46–55

From an early age Mary would have been taught the Scriptures. This rich knowledge of the Bible is present in her song, which is saturated with Old Testament language. Mary would also have been influenced by the social conditions of her day. She lived in a land occupied by enemy soldiers, among the common people there was grinding poverty, and an oppressive taxation system bred resentment against rich landowners. Mary was a genuine representative of the poor underclass, and she weaves these personal circumstances into her song. Mary first expresses her joy and gratitude to God for His surprising grace to a lowly woman. The reason that generations of believers have called Mary a blessed disciple is because of her humility and faith in the greatness of God (Luke 1:46–48). Mary then praises the power of God and likens Him to a Mighty Commander rescuing a beleaguered people. He performs mighty deeds, He scatters the proud, He deposes rulers, He sends rich people away empty handed (vv.49–53). And Mary rejoices in God as her Merciful Helper. He extends His mercy to those who fear Him, He lifts the humble, He fills the hungry with good things, He helps needy people, He remembers to keep His promises (vv.50–55).

The revolutionary message of the *Magnificat* would be fulfilled by Jesus in His ministry. He encountered the religious rulers of the day, who tried to trap Him with their legalistic questioning, but by His teaching, Jesus exposed foolish thinking and scattered pride. Jesus challenged the greed of the rich and powerful who marginalised the poor and hungry. Through His miracles He healed the sick, fed the hungry and restored the fortunes of the poor.

It is a remarkable sign of God's grace and power in Mary's life that the Holy Spirit should inspire in this young woman a song of such deep wisdom. The *Magnificat* reaches back into the history of God's people, takes account of the times in which Mary is living, expresses a rich understanding of God's saving work as a Mighty Deliverer and

Merciful Helper, anticipates the ministry of Jesus, who would bring good news to the poor and oppressed, and stretches forward to a future when God the Judge will overturn the kingdoms of this world and establish His eternal kingdom.

Pause for thought
Why is Mary's song so full of past tense phrases? Look at the number of times she uses the phrase 'He has'. Does this mean she is only referring to what God has done in the past?

No, Mary is expressing a faith in God which is timelessly true. She is so confident that God will do what He has promised. Her song foresees the final judgment of God, when there will be a complete reversal of a system ruled by human values and the world will be ruled by our righteous King.

Prayer for today
Pray the following prayer based on Revelation 21:4 and 22:20. Pray it in the knowledge that God's plans are already in motion, and with the faith that He will accomplish all He has promised.

Lord, thank You
For wiping every tear from our eyes
Thank You for the gift of a new heaven and new earth
Thank You that there there are no funeral services
No grieving families
No tears of the oppressed
No cries of the poor
Praise You for deposing the old order and establishing Your everlasting kingdom
Amen and amen!

Reflection
Mary is open but not gullible; overawed but not intimidated; obedient but not passive; not a doormat but a willing doorway for 'the Lord Christ to enter in'.[1]

17 Dec

The *Benedictus*

Bible passage
Luke 1:67–79

Nick Page, has written a hilarious book on worship songs, *Now Let's Move into a Time of Nonsense*.[2] In it he confesses that at one time he had problems with the strange imagery of Charles Wesley's 'Hark the Herald Angels Sing', especially the lines: 'Hail the Sun of Righteousness! … Light and life to all he brings, Risen with healing in his wings.'

I will leave you to discover what he thought the lines meant![3] He suggests it would be good if one Christmas someone explained any cryptic carol lyrics to the congregation. After Nick had studied the Bible he realised that there were Old Testament writers such as Malachi who used the imagery of the rising sun (Mal. 4:2). This helped Nick understand that Charles Wesley was saying that Jesus rises like the sun and His coming to earth heralds the dawn of a new day.

In our reading today, we find Zechariah using the same imagery of the rising sun and, in addition, puzzling phrases like 'a horn of salvation'. So what do these cryptic words mean?

Zechariah had a significant ministry but he had much to learn about walking with God. Because of his unbelief, he lived for nine months in a silent world which gave him time to ponder his faith and examine the Scriptures. When the day came for him to name his newly born son, he scrawled the name 'John' on a writing tablet (v.63) and his speech was restored. If his faith had been weakened by a bad memory of God's promises, his faith was restored by recalling those same ancient words.

Although Zechariah was the proud father of John, his song focuses on the unborn baby Jesus. He offers his praise to God for visiting and redeeming His people! He praises God for remembering the words He had spoken through the prophets (vv.70–71). God's gift of Jesus is described as the raising of 'a horn of salvation'. A horned ox is a symbol of overwhelming strength (Deut. 33:17) and a sign of God's determination to overcome His enemies (2 Sam. 22:3; Psa. 18:2). Zechariah prophesies that the Messiah will have the strength and power to deliver His people from all who hate them (v.71). This Saviour will bring a total deliverance, enabling God's people to serve Him 'all their days' without fear (vv.74–75).

The arrival of Jesus would be like the dawning of a new day (v.78). The rising of this Sun would come quietly and imperceptibly, so silent that the wider world would not be aware that God was 'imparting to human hearts the blessings of His heaven'.

Pause for thought
Can you imagine Zechariah one day explaining to his young son the meaning of the *Benedictus?* 'My dear son John, a prophetic ministry awaits you. God has called you to prepare the way for the One who will be *the* Way. You will point people to Him who will bring salvation and forgiveness of sins. You will declare that because of God's tender mercy the Sun will rise from heaven. This rising Sun will banish the darkness of death. And lead us on a journey of peace.'

Prayer for today
> God of faithfulness and truth
> You sent Your servant John the Baptist
> To preach in the desert
> And summon the people to repentance
> Make us and all things new
> That in the wilderness of our hearts
> We too may prepare a way
> Over which Your Son may walk

Reflection
A grandmother was sitting with her grandchildren on a mountainside, watching a magnificent sunrise. She said to them, 'Pray that God will shine the light of hope and healing into every home in the valley below.'

Jesus tells us that as His disciples today, we are to be lights in this dark world, illuminating the path to God for those who cannot yet see it.

18 Dec

The *Nunc Dimitis*

Bible passage
Luke 2:25–35

I once heard a radio interview with a man called Kevin O'Connell. He has worked as a sound re-recording mixer on many great soundtracks, including those of the award-winning films *Terms of Endearment, Top Gun* and *A Few Good Men*. Since 1983 he has been nominated for an Oscar for best soundtrack twenty times, but to date has failed to achieve first place. When asked what it would mean to win after years of nominations, Kevin replied: 'It would prove to the world that you should never give up on your dreams, regardless how difficult it might be.'

The Bible does not tell us anything about the feelings of Simeon on the day his dreams were realised. His reward for waiting was not an Oscar for patience but a gift of grace because of his faith.

It had been revealed to Simeon by the Holy Spirit that he would not die until he had seen the Christ (v.26). Because the coming of Jesus was carefully choreographed by God, we should not be surprised that Simeon is led by the Holy Spirit to arrive at the Temple as Mary and Joseph are bringing their newborn baby for presentation (v.27).

Simeon was 'waiting for the consolation of Israel' (v.25). This was a phrase which originated in the writings of Isaiah, and spoke of the arrival of the messianic age when God would comfort His people.

How remarkable that this pious believer is anointed with the Holy Spirit to say a prayer of blessing over baby Jesus. Simeon's words imply that this child is the answer to a lifetime of prayers. But the startling revelation is that the child Jesus is destined to be the Saviour of the whole world, not just the Jewish nation. No wonder this announcement produced amazement in the parents (v.33).

There are three themes in Simeon's song of joy which centre around Jesus. First, that *God's promise is fulfilled in Jesus* (v.29). Simeon is like a guard on duty watching for the arrival of an expected event. With the coming of Jesus the waiting is over and

Simeon now asks permission to leave his post.

Simeon's second theme tells is that *God's salvation has arrived in Jesus* (vv.30–31). In seeing the baby Jesus, Simeon exclaims he has seen the salvation which God has been carefully preparing. As Luke unfolds his story, the salvation which comes through Jesus becomes plain.

Third, *God's light appears in the Person of Jesus* (vv.32–33). The Light of the World now shines for the largest audience imaginable – Jews and Gentiles. To the Jews, the coming of the Light would be glory for Israel. By the arrival of Jesus the nation of Israel is vindicated in the eyes of the world (Isa. 60:3; Matt 2:1–2). To the Gentiles, Jesus the Light will be a revelation. They too will be included in the salvation story in ways they could never have imagined.

Pause for thought
Can each one of us be a disciple like Simeon: a mind shaped by the Scriptures; a faith focused on the promises of God; a life choreographed by the Holy Spirit?

Prayer for today
Lord we seek your consolation.
We wait for your coming.
We long for your promised comfort.
O come desire of the nations.
O come O come Immanuel.[4]

Reflection
Consider the number of times in these verses there is mention of the Holy Spirit working in the prayer life of Simeon. There was nothing trivial about his prayers. We may pray for a parking place at the supermarket and fine weather at half-term, but Simeon's prayer life was focused unselfishly on God's promises being fulfilled in the wider world. Ask God to show you today those places in the world where He is working out His promises.

19 Dec

The *Gloria*

Bible passage
Luke 2:14

'Angel voices ever singing' is one of the most joyful of the older songs in the hymnbook. Consider these words from the first verse:

> Angel voices ever singing
> Round Thy throne of light,
> Angel harps for ever ringing,
> Rest not day nor night;
> Thousands only live to bless Thee,
> And confess Thee
> Lord of might.
>
> Francis Pott (1832–1909)

The hymnwriter has captured here the essence of how the Bible describes the joyful worship of heaven. When we gather for worship we are joining the angels and the archangels and all the company of heaven in proclaiming the great and glorious name of our Holy God (Heb. 12:22).

Angels are mentioned over 100 times in the Old Testament and more than 160 times in the New Testament. The word 'angel' means 'God's messenger', and angels exist in vast numbers (Rev. 5:11).

At his commission, Isaiah saw winged seraphim and heard the sound of choral singing echoing around God's throne room as the angels proclaimed: 'Holy, holy, holy is the LORD Almighty; the whole earth is full of his glory' (Isa. 6:3). Daniel, in his awesome vision, saw the 'Ancient of Days', God, sitting down on His throne, with thousands of angels attending Him and standing before Him (Dan. 7:9–10). John, in his magnificent description of heavenly worship, also speaks of a choir of angels singing with a loud voice: 'Worthy is the Lamb, who was slain, to receive power and wealth and wisdom and strength and honour and glory and praise!' (Rev. 5:11–12).

In our passage today, we find that when the eternal Word lay as a baby in a straw-filled feeding trough, the loud choral anthem from the angels was 'Glory to God in the highest ...' (Luke 2:14). God chose singers from His vast angel choir to appear to some poor shepherds working the nightshift in the fields outside Bethlehem. In the first sermon Jesus preached He said He was anointed to preach good news to the poor. On the night Jesus was born, the heavenly choir led the way in bringing that good news to the poor.

Pause for thought
'Glory to God in the highest, and on earth peace to men on whom his favour rests.' The message of the angels is clear – when God is given His rightful place of pre-eminence in the universe there is peace on earth to all those who respond positively to the coming of Jesus.

Prayer for today
> Great and glorious God
> We sing joyfully with Your heavenly choir
> The Lord reigns!
> Let the earth rejoice!
> Let the coastlands be glad!
> Let the peoples praise You!
> Let the nations be glad and sing for joy!
> Let the oppressed see it and be glad!
> Let all who seek You rejoice and be glad in You!
> May those who love Your salvation say evermore –
> God is great!

Inspired by Psalms 97, 67, 69 and 70

Reflection
Status in the eyes of the world may be associated with money, property and social standing. God does not recognise these categories when He wants to include people in the good news of Jesus. God chose to send His angel choir to ordinary shepherds without any status, and He has chosen to reveal Himself to you – whoever you are. God's gift of Jesus is the means to qualify you to be used greatly in His kingdom.

20 Dec

The Servant King

Bible passage
Philippians 2:1–18

The following words, attacking new styles of church music, appeared in a newspaper article: 'The new Christian music is not as pleasant as the more established style, because there are so many new songs, you can't learn them all. It puts too much emphasis on instrumental music rather than Godly lyrics. The preceding generation got on perfectly well without it.'[5] The article was written in 1723 as an attack on the composing skills of Isaac Watts, the writer of 'When I survey the wondrous cross'!

There is nothing new about conflict in the Church. Two thousand years ago, the church at Philippi was in danger of allowing disagreements to destroy their unity in Christ (Phil. 2:2–4; 4:2). There were bad attitudes of selfish pride and ambition, and Paul counters these with a song that captures the wonder of Christ's humility, which is the pattern of behaviour for those He came to save.

Before Bethlehem, Jesus shared with the Father the glory of heaven before the world began (John 17:5). But Jesus never considered equality with God something to be held on to at all costs. In order 'to clothe another in fine raiment, love lays aside its own imperial robe'.[6] At Bethlehem, the One who had inhabited the place of perfection was born in a borrowed stable. He who experienced the worship of heaven would be despised and rejected by human beings. In the Upper Room, He who could command legions of angels in His service takes the towel and basin and washes the dirty feet of His disciples. On the cross at Calvary, He who had stooped to our mortality stoops lower to the ignominy of the shame and suffering for our sin. 'He who flung stars into space, to cruel nails surrendered.'[7]

But God has exalted Jesus and given Him the highest status in the universe. Our proudest titles are nothing compared to His. Jesus is the Name above all names.

The coronation of Jesus has already taken place. Jesus is King! But

God has planned a day when the 'incognito King' will be universally seen and acknowledged. 'The lovers of Jesus know it and rejoice, but the world's millions do not know that Jesus is King. But they will on the day the King comes.'[8]

Pause for thought

Look at the words of the worship song in Philippians 2 and consider the pastoral challenge. Paul says to a local congregation: 'Each of you should look ... to the interests of others' (v.4) and 'Do everything without complaining or arguing ...' (v.14). When our worship is full of praise to the heavenly King who became the helpless baby, our life of service will be shaped by His attitude of humility. When everyone else was quarrelling about status, Jesus took the towel and basin.

Prayer for today

> Lord, I can't pray for the sins of the whole Church
> But I can offer my own prayer of confession
> Where I have been corrupt, purge me
> Where I have been in error, direct me
> Where I have been wrong, correct me
> Where I have been hard, soften me
> Help me now to focus on You, my Saviour
> Jesus, rescue me from the mess of church conflict
> Jesus, restore me to my brothers and sisters in faith
> Jesus, grant me Your mind and attitude
> Use me in Your peace-making and bridge-building service
> Through Christ the King
> Amen

Reflection

The clear indication is that a local church is prospering when unity is prevailing. The contribution each member can make to the harmony of the fellowship is to focus on the same things, possess the same love and aim for the same purpose.

21 Dec

Song of supremacy

Bible passage
Colossians 1:15–20

This Christmas, whether you visit shops to purchase gifts or buy online, you will encounter thousands of advertising messages. Our thinking all too easily falls in line with the advertiser's aim: If you want to be 'with it' you can't be seen without our product.

When the early disciples were wrestling with how to be faithful followers of Jesus Christ, they too were bombarded with conflicting messages and images. The image of the Roman emperor was as familiar to them as the advertising logos of today are to us. In the marketplace coins, jewellery and drinking goblets all conveyed the same message: Caesar is the Lord and he reigns on high.

The church at Colosse sung a different song to the marketplace. It is possible that the verses we have read today were originally a three-verse song of supremacy to Jesus Christ. The theme of this worship song was counter cultural – *Jesus* is the Lord and He reigns on high.

Paul's discipleship teaching was tailor-made for everyday living. He shared with the young believers: 'So then, just as you received Christ Jesus as Lord, continue to live in him …' (Col. 2:6). If they wanted to be effective and fruitful as followers of Jesus, they had to be subversive for disciples. The images of Caesar were false and delusory; their identity as Christians had to be shaped by the message and the image of Jesus Christ. This was Paul's message. First, that *Christ Jesus is the image of the invisible God* (Col. 1:15). God by nature is invisible until He reveals Himself, and He has done this fully in Jesus. The God who brought the world into being was born as a helpless baby in Bethlehem. Jesus living among us as a human being – He is the only One we are to model our lives on.

Second, *the entire universe came into being through Christ Jesus* (v.16). It is mind-boggling to realise that the God who made the wealth of the cosmos cares for you. Total security is not found in the wealth of property or investments.

Third, *Christ Jesus is the great Sustainer of everything He has made* (v.17). Everything holds together in Him. Remove His sustaining power and the universe would implode. If the sustaining power of the Lord keeps the cosmos in place, then surely He is able to keep you from falling.

Fourth, *Christ Jesus is the Head of the Church and the pioneer of all new beginnings* (v.18). There was a new beginning on the first day of creation, on the first Easter Day and on the day of Pentecost, and Christ Jesus pioneers a new beginning every time a person comes into a living relationship with Him. If you are looking for newness in your life, don't expect to obtain it through a commodity you purchase. You are a brand-new creation in Christ and His creative power is renewed in you day by day (2 Cor. 5:17; Lam. 3:22–23).

And fifth, *because the fullness of God dwells in Christ Jesus, He is the world's supreme Reconciler* (vv.19–20). The broken pieces of our lives cannot be mended by a shopping expedition or a move of location. Brokenness can only be transformed into beauty because Jesus shed His blood on the cross.

Pause for thought
Christ is the image of the invisible God. This is the image and message that should be shaping our lives daily. We were not created to be perpetual shoppers and consumers of commodities. In a world where we are bombarded with images, Jesus Christ is the image *par excellence*. Only His life in us can provide us with a fulfilling identity.

Prayer for today
Lord Jesus, I want Your image alone to be the logo of my life
Show me the deadly dangers of worshipping at false altars
I celebrate Your eternal glory power and wealth.
Help me always to use Your gifts of creation for Your pleasure alone
In your strength
Amen

Reflection
Worship songs in praise of Jesus Christ are not only for Sunday in the sanctuary, but also Monday in the shopping mall.

Suggestion for group activity – Week Three

Carols by the fireside

Host a 'Carols by the Fireside' evening. Invite neighbours and friends to share the joy of Christmas in the intimate setting of a home. Begin the celebration with drinks and snacks.

In advance of the evening, invite five or six people to choose their favourite carol and prepare a short presentation about how the carol came to be written. After each presentation, sing each carol together.

To conclude the evening you could read the following thoughtful excerpt which captures the staggering truth of the incarnation. It is from J.B. Phillips' *The Visited Planet*. Philips imagines a senior angel showing a very young angel around the splendours of the universe. They view whirling galaxies and blazing suns until at last they enter one particular galaxy of 500 billion stars:

As the two of them drew near to the star we call our sun and to its circling planets, the senior angel pointed to a small and rather insignificant sphere turning very slowly on its axis. It looked as dull as a dirty tennis ball to the little angel, whose mind was filled with the size and glory of what he had seen. 'I want you to watch that one particularly', said the senior angel pointing with his finger. 'Well it looks very small and dirty to me', said the little angel, 'what's so special about that one?'

To the little angel earth did not seem very impressive. He listened in stunned disbelief as the senior angel told him that this small planet, insignificant and not very clean, was the visited planet. 'Do you mean that our great and glorious Prince ... went down in person to this fifth rate ball? Why should he do a thing like that?' ... The little angel's voice wrinkled in disgust. 'Do you mean to tell me', he said, 'that he stooped so low as to become one of those creeping crawling creatures of that floating ball?'

'I do, and I don't think that he would like you to call them "creeping crawling creatures" in that tone of voice. For strange as it may seem to us, He loves them. He went down to visit them to lift them up to become like him.'

The little angel looked blank. Such a thought was almost beyond his comprehension.[9]

Music resources

If you want a new slant on traditional carols then look at the material in *New Carol Praise*, edited by David Peacock and Noel Tredinnick (London: HarperCollins, 2006). The CD that comes with the book includes twenty-six songs which you can download from www.missionpraise.com

If you visit Graham Kendrick's website you can download his Christmas album *Dreaming of a Holy Night* (Make Way Music/Fierce!, 2007). You can also download a virtual songbook of the album's songs, including both the words and the music. Graham's other Christmas albums are available from this website too. Visit www.grahamkendrick.co.uk

For a more folk-style approach to carols, look at *Carols and Capers* by Maddy Prior and the Carnival Band (Park Records, 2007). Visit www.maddyprior.co.uk or download from iTunes.

Other websites with resource material for Christmas include: The General Board of Discipleship website – www.gbod.org/worship (ideas for Advent); The Text This Week website – www.textweek.com (preaching ideas, movie clips, suggestions on the theme and a picture database).

1. Philip Greenslade, *The Perfect Gift: The birth of Jesus – the turning point of history* (Farnham: CWR, 2002) p.77.
2. Nick Page, *And Now Let's Move into a Time of Nonsense: Why worship songs are failing the Church* (Authentic Media, 2004).
3. Ibid., pp.84-86.
4. Christopher J. Ellis and Myra Blyth for the Baptist Union of Great Britain, *Gathering for Worship: Patterns and Prayers for the Community of Disciples* (Norwich: Canterbury Press, 2005) p.354. Used by permission.
5. Interview with Tim Hughes in 'UK Focus', *Alpha News* newspaper (January, 2006) p.7.
6. J.H. Jowett, *The High Calling* (London: Andrew Melrose Covent Garden, 1910) p.64.
7. Graham Kendrick, 'The Servant King' (Eastbourne: Make Way Music, 1983).
8. Alec Motyer, *The Message of Philippians* (Leicester: IVP, 1984) p.122.
9. J.B. Phillips, *New Testament Christianity* (London: Hodder & Stoughton, 1958) pp.27–33.

Saviour of Joy

In this fourth week of readings we will focus on the Saviour of joy, Jesus, and we will use the 'prologue' of John's Gospel for our daily meditations.

The prologue (John 1:1–18) is almost like the overture of a musical, in which we hear excerpts of the main songs that will be played in the rest of the performance. Similarly, in the first eighteen verses of John, we can hear snatches of the main melodies of the life of Jesus, which unfold with full harmony in the following chapters of this Gospel.

John's story of Jesus takes us back to *before* the beginning of time. Using language that will help his readers to understand the story of Jesus, John says that the Word (Jesus) had no beginning of His own – when other things began, He already was. The Word has an eternal relationship with God. The Word is divine in Himself, as the Father is. The Word is life-giving and light-bearing. The Christmas message rests on this incredible truth: the Word became flesh; the child in the manger was God.

Back to before the beginning

Bible passage
John 1:1–2

John is in a class of his own when it comes to commencing his Gospel. He is like an eagle that soars higher than anything and has the vision to see that the beginning of the good news story precedes the beginning of the universe.

The real beginning was when nothing existed except God. John's opening words in his Gospel are a deliberate reminder of the first verses of the Bible, where we read that the earth was formless and darkness overshadowed everything. The book of Genesis begins with creation, and John refers to creation too (John 1:3–5). Very soon he will address the issue of new birth (John 3:1–21), what the Bible calls 'new creation' (2 Cor. 5:17).

It was revealed to John that the Word speaking on the first morning of creation was the Word Jesus Christ. When God spoke the words: 'Let there be light and there was light' (Genesis 1:3) these creative words were uttered by Jesus Christ the Word of God.

John says three things about the Word of God. First, the Word existed co-equally with God. Although Jesus was born as a Man and lived in a specific time period, He is not bound by time. There was never a time when the Word did not exist.

Second, the Word shared God's eternal glory before the world began (John 17:24). The phrase 'the Word was with God' can be translated 'the Word was face to face with God'. This rendering emphasises the distinct existence of the Word.

Third, the Word was God. This means that when we hear and see the words and deeds of Jesus, we are hearing and seeing the words and deeds of God.

Pause for thought

Like John, we need to reflect deeply on the Scriptures and receive the ministry of Jesus for today. When Jesus speaks His words of comfort, our burdens are lighter (Matt. 11:28–30). When Jesus speaks words of prophetic wisdom, our lives are given a new direction (John 4:16–19). When Jesus makes promises, we should expect His Holy Spirit to be guiding our lives (John 16:13).

Prayer for today

Lord, speak a clear word into my life today
Reveal to me where I am carrying too heavy a burden
Challenge my lifestyle with your perfect wisdom
Guide me every step of today by the presence of Your Holy Spirit

Reflection

John said he wrote his Gospel to strengthen our faith in Jesus (John 20:31). Look at Jesus in the manger and say, 'You were born for me.' Look at the Saviour on the cross and say, 'You died for me.' Look at the Christ who ascended and say, 'You rose for me.' Look at the Lord who reigns and waits and say, 'You will return for me.' Now go out and serve the Lord today in the power of the Holy Spirit!

23 Dec

Why care about creation?

Bible passage
John 1:3–5

The year was 1974. The place, the headquarters of The Royal Society in London, an organisation made up of eminent scientists, engineers and technologists. The occasion, the annual election of Fellows of The Royal Society. Each year, The Society elects forty-four new Fellows and six new Foreign Members, chosen for their scientific achievements. Gaining one of these titles is the highest accolade a scientist can receive next to a Nobel Prize.

At the front of the room, a young man in a wheelchair signed his

name slowly in a very large book, which on an earlier page bore
the name of a former Fellow and President of The Society – Sir Isaac
Newton. The young man in the wheelchair was Stephen Hawking.
His bestselling book *A Brief History of Time* has gone into ten
editions, has been translated into thirty languages and has sold more
than nine million copies. The book is considered by many to be a
classic 'unread bestseller' – many people own it and have started it,
but few have finished.

Those who have the stamina to read to the end of Hawking's
book will discover he has much to say about a unifying principle
to explain the mystery of life. He concludes: 'Ever since the dawn
of civilization, people have not been content to see events as
unconnected and inexplicable. They have craved an understanding
of the underlying order in the world. Today we still yearn to know
why we are here and where we came from.'[1]

John, inspired by the Holy Spirit, provides us with a theological
response to Hawking. He declares that Jesus is the unifying principle
that explains the universe: 'Through him all things were made ...'
(John 1:3). Jesus Christ is the One who reveals the underlying order
in the world. Everything that exists has its origin, purpose and unity
in Jesus Christ (Col. 1:16).

The Bible opens with the story of creation, when life and light came
into being. In the incarnation God comes 'up close and personal'.
Revelation in creation has become revelation in the incarnation.

In the birth of Jesus we are invited to marvel at the glory of God
as a tiny infant with soft baby flesh. This child is the source of our
light and life. He is the Saviour who will be the giver of eternal life
to those who believe in Him (John 3:16) and the bestower of light to
those who follow Him (John 8:12).

Pause for thought
Why should we care about creation? We should care because
everything we see is the handiwork of Jesus the Word. A lack of
concern for creation reveals a very limited view of Jesus Christ.

Why should we care about evangelism? We should care because
every human being derives their life from God, in whom 'we live
and move and have our being' (Acts 17:28).

Prayer for today
May the light of the glorious gospel of Christ
Shine into the hearts of all Your people
And reveal Your glory
Amen

Reflection
As you tackle the problems of today, remember Jesus is the ultimate source of everything. All things hold together in Him.

Ask the Lord to be fully involved in the challenges you are facing.

24 Dec

A reliable witness

Bible passage
John 1:6–9

My wife and I were visiting Peru for ministry meetings and flew from Lima to the old colonial city of Cajamarca, which is 9,000 feet above sea level. Here we succumbed to altitude sickness (or, as one of our grandchildren mistakenly pronounced it, 'attitude sickness'!) and we were out of action for twenty-four hours.

Cajamarca is noted for a decisive moment in the demise of the Inca Empire. In November 1532 the Spanish conquistadors encountered the Inca Emperor Atahualpa in the town square. The Spanish friar offered the Inca chief a copy of the four Gospels and said it was God's Word and that through these Scriptures God's voice could be heard.

Reputedly, the Inca chief put the book to his ear and said he could not hear God's voice. He threw the Gospels on the ground. The Spanish saw this action as an insult to Christianity and their troops immediately opened fire. Seven thousand Indians were killed, the Inca Emperor was captured and the course of Latin American history was changed forever.

Mission by bullets has never advanced God's work. Mission by loving witness never fails. When we focus on witnessing to Christ the Light of the World, we should expect that people will come to believe through our witness (John 1:6–7).

'Witness' was a favourite word of John's. Just as in a court of law witnesses may be called to support a case, so John calls various witnesses to verify the truth of the case for Christ. When we examine the comprehensive nature of John's witness to Jesus, we realise the reliability of what John the Baptist said of Christ. He declared that Jesus is 'the Lamb of God, who takes away the sin of the world!' (John 1:29). Jesus is the Bridegroom who will bring great joy to the bride's heart (the Church) when He arrives (John 3:28–29). Jesus is the true Light of the World (John 5:35–36). Jesus must become increasingly greater while we become increasingly less in focus (John 3:30). Jesus is the One who will baptise His disciples with the Holy Spirit and with fire (Luke 3:16). Jesus and His kingdom need careful preparation. Our lives are like roads that have to be straightened and levelled (Luke 3:4–14).

Pause for thought
The ultimate test of a reliable witness is that he is believed. People professed that everything John the Baptist told them about Jesus was true and reliable and many people believed in Jesus through his witness (John 10:41–42).

Prayer for today
Living God,
as we remember John the Baptist
who by his integrity, prepared the way for Jesus,
and every other faithful witness
who has stood by your truth
whatever the cost,
make us faithful
to the truth we know,
so that by our integrity
we may prepare the way for Jesus
into many lives,
to the honour of your name.[2]

Reflection

By your words and actions you can have a 'John the Baptist ministry' today. As you meet family, friends and work colleagues, you will see the potholes of knowledge that need to be filled in with good news. You will notice the crooked paths that need straightening with godly wisdom. 'John the Baptist ministry' prepares the way for Jesus to do His greater work in people's lives.

25 Dec

No room

Bible passages
Luke 2:6–7; John 1:10–11

It's Christmas Day. Today, the well-known carols and Bible readings will be at the heart of worship celebrations around the world. Some of us barely need to see the words, they are so familiar. But let's consider the following phrase in more detail: 'because there was no room for them in the inn' (Luke 2:7).

I have preached many Christmas Day sermons on the over-crowded Bethlehem, the hardhearted innkeeper who turns the young couple away, Mary and Joseph finding the stable at the back of the inn, and in this lowly setting the baby Jesus being born. The spiritual application is plain. Would the innkeeper have responded differently if he had known the identity of the unborn baby? Unlike the innkeeper, will we make room for Jesus in the midst of our Christmas celebrations?

But let's note what the Bible actually says. First, there is no hint of the urgency of Mary's impending labour. Luke simply records that Joseph and Mary arrived in Bethlehem and while they were there the time came for the baby to be born (2:6). Second, there is no mention of a conversation between Joseph and an innkeeper. Third, the word 'inn', in the sense of a pub with rooms for rent, may not be a good translation of the original Greek text. The Greek word used here, *katalyma*, can be translated in three possible ways: 'inn', 'house' or 'guest room'. Luke refers to a commercial inn in the story of the Good Samaritan (Luke 10:34) but he uses the word *pandocheion*. It is more likely that the word *katalyma* refers to a guestroom in a large family house. So, Mary and Joseph may have found hospitality in a crowded house where the guestroom (the inn) was already occupied.

We could imagine that when the time came for Mary to give birth to Jesus, she moved from the crowded family room to a quieter lower level space, shared by some animals, and it was here that she gave birth to Jesus. In this part of the house the newborn child is laid in the comfort of a hay-filled manger.

This plain reading of Scripture may remove the picture of an innkeeper shutting the door on Mary and Joseph; instead it focuses on Jesus being born in the normal setting of a crowded family home, 'with the oxen standing by'.

Pause for thought

The world makes no room for Jesus (v.10). He was in the world but the world failed to recognise Him. The world was made through Him but it fails to acknowledge its Maker. The world has no desire to know Him.

And yet Jesus came. He lived, died and rose again to make it possible for His enemies to be His friends.

Prayer for today

Lord Jesus Christ
Born in love in a lowly stable
I kneel in wonder at Your amazing grace
Make my life an open door of obedient service
And give me strength to serve You with joy
All the days of my life
To the honour and glory of Your name
Amen

Reflection

Take time to think about how others are spending Christmas Day. For some this will be the first Christmas without a loved one, and the burden of bereavement will still be heavy. Some will find a large noisy family celebration overwhelming and fall apart with the extra pressure. In parts of the world public demonstrations of Christmas joy are illegal. There will be those who have been physically threatened because they are followers of Jesus. As names and situations come to your mind, follow up these thoughts with an encouraging email, a phone call or a visit. After the presents have been opened, the season of giving continues (2 Cor. 8:9).

26 Dec

How you become a member of God's family

Bible passages
John 1:12–13; 3:1–21

I am part of a local Christian community in which the birth of a new baby is always celebrated with great joy. The congregation want all the details. How much did the baby weigh? What are the names of the child? What family likeness is there?

In the Gospels it is extraordinary that for all the focus on the birth of Jesus, we have very few details of the baby. As Jane Williams observes: 'We are not told what he looked like or whether he was a particularly good baby. Did he feed well? Did he sleep well? How did he react to his odd visitors? What colour were his eyes? We know none of these things. He was just a baby.'[3]

John spares us the details and allows the significance of the unique birth of Jesus to be a reflection for our spiritual birth as children of God. We have learnt from Luke's account of the unique conception of Mary's child – that no human decision was involved. John makes this same point again (v.13).

If being born into God's family is quite different from being born into a human family (John 3:6), then how do we enter the heavenly family?

We are not born into God's family by physical birth. Some people believe that having the correct bloodline is all you need to be assured of a place in God's family. We catch a glimpse of this in Paul's testimony when he lists his impeccable pedigree (Phil. 3:5). Similarly today, you may belong to an impeccable family of Christian believers but this does not qualify you to be part of God's family.

Neither are we born into God's family by human emotions or

desires. Natural appetites and emotions are in play when a child is conceived, but you cannot simply wish or hope you are part of God's family.

And we are not born into God's family by effort and determination. The reference to a husband's will (v.13) is a reflection that in the time of John it was expected that the male took the lead in sexual matters. It was by a husband's initiative that a child was conceived. John states you may get many things in life by sheer determination but you cannot become a child of God by this method.

So how can a person be born into the family of God? By the sheer miracle of God's gift of grace. By receiving Jesus and believing on His name.

Pause for thought

How silently, how silently,
The wondrous gift is given!
So God imparts to human hearts
The blessings of his heaven.
No ear may hear his coming;
But in this world of sin,
Where meek souls will receive him, still
The dear Christ enters in.[4]

Prayer for today

Lord Jesus
By Your birth, death and resurrection the path to life has been opened to us
Help us to walk Your way with greater trust
Teach us to accept Your truth with greater faith
Prompt us to share Your life with greater generosity
For the honour and glory of Your name
Amen

Reflection

God first plants within our heart what we might call the ovum of saving faith, for we are told that even faith is not of ourselves, it is 'the gift of God' (Eph. 2:8). Second, he sends forth the seed of his Word, which contains the divine life within it, to pierce the ovum of faith. The result is conception. Thus, a new spiritual life comes into being, a life that has its origin in God ...[5]

27 Dec

Miracle in the stable

Bible passage
John 1:14

Our verse today stands as one of the most important in the Bible. It is stupendous in what it claims: the Word became flesh. The Word that spoke and a universe came into being became a child without speech. The Word that flung stars into space became flesh and surrendered His hands to cruel nails. The Word through whom the world was made laid aside His glory and took on flesh.

'Flesh' means human nature in all its weakness and all its liability to sin. Some people believe Jesus only seemed human. They believe that wherever He walked He left no footprint, that He was never hungry and tired and that He could not possibly get tangled up with the mess of human flesh and personality. But the Bible says it is a heresy to believe this. One of the tests of a true prophet is that he confess Jesus Christ came to earth in the flesh (1 John 4:2).

The truth is that Jesus wore our humanity but without our sin. John is clear that he has seen with his own eyes the Word living as a fleshly human being, and he has one word to describe this fleshly life of Jesus: glory!

This glory was seen when Jesus turned the water into wine (John 2:1–11). It was seen again when Jesus healed an army commander's son from a distance (4:43–54). It was glory when a man who had been unwell for thirty-eight years was healed (5:1–15). Glory is seen in the miracle of the feeding of five thousand people (6:1–15). There was more glory when Jesus healed a blind man (9:1–12). The family of Lazarus saw the glory of God because they believed that their dead brother would rise from the dead (11:17–44).

Six times John records that he saw the glory of God in the fleshly ministry of Jesus.

The seventh sign of glory was when the Word that had become flesh died on the cross. John remembers that Jesus predicted this moment of His ultimate revelation of glory (12:23–28).

Pause for thought

Christmas can only be understood as a worship experience. The only place to comprehend the meaning 'the Word became flesh' is on our knees in worship. Ponder on our verse for today again: 'The Word became flesh and made his dwelling among us.' This is the birth of our Saviour who fully identifies with us in our human condition and will do so all the way to the cross. This is the birth of our Friend who, like no one else, understands the burdens we carry (Matt. 11:28).

Prayer for today

O source of all good,
What shall I render to thee for the gift of gifts,
Thine own dear Son, begotten, not created,
my redeemer, proxy, surety, substitute,
his self-emptying incomprehensible,
His infinity of love beyond the heart's grasp.
Herein is wonder of wonders:
He came below to raise me above,
Was born like me that I might become like Him …
In Him thou hast given me so much
That heaven can give no more.[6]

Reflection

The Word became flesh, so Jesus understands what it means to live as a human being. He knows what it is to be tired and weary (John 4:6); He too has wept over the sin of an unbelieving community (Luke 19:41); He cried at the graveside of a dear friend (John 11:35); He was angry with His disciples when they failed to see the place of children in His kingdom (Mark 10:14–15); He too has been tempted and understands our trials and temptations (Luke 22:44; Heb. 4:15); He knows the exhilaration of joy and wants us to experience this human emotion in its fullness (John 15:11; 17:13).

28 Dec

Up close and personal

Bible passage
John 1:15–18

Of all the books by Philip Yancey, I have found *Reaching for the Invisible God* to be one of the most intellectually satisfying and pastorally helpful. I have used passages from this book to assist friends who are struggling with what they would term 'baffling providence'.

When Yancey was concluding the manuscript of this book, he sent an early draft to a variety of readers for their comments. One of these readers wrote back:

> So be of good courage, my friend, and let this book be what every religious book is, an imperfect finger pointing with an indeterminable accuracy towards Someone we cannot by our pointing make present, but Someone from whom and toward whom we nonetheless feel permission to point, feebly, laughably, tenderly.[7]

John points with a perfect finger to the truth that no one has ever seen (the invisible) God at any time (John 1:18). Moses was a very important person in the communication of God's Law (v.17) but when he saw the Lord's glory he was not allowed to see God's face, for God said 'no-one may see me and live' (Exod. 33:20). The vision that Isaiah had of the Holy God nearly destroyed him (Isa. 6:5). People had their partial glimpses of God, but none of these Old Testament encounters revealed God's essential being.

Then the Word became flesh. The invisible God made Himself visible as a human being. The Almighty God appeared on earth as a helpless human baby. Jesus was like any new born baby needing to be fed, changed and eventually taught to walk and talk. As Jim Packer says: 'The more you think about it, the more staggering it gets. Nothing in fiction is so fantastic as is this truth of the incarnation.'[8]

John is in no doubt about what happened in the Bethlehem manger: 'No-one has ever seen God, but God the One and Only, who is at the Father's side, has made him known' (John 1:18).

The reference to the Father's side is a most intimate expression. In some translations the image is of resting on someone's bosom. The expression is found in the story of the Rich Man and Lazarus, when Lazarus dies and the angels carry him to Abraham's side (Luke 16:22). It is also used to describe the beloved disciple John reclining at Jesus' side at the Last Supper (John 13:23). The Father's side conveys an image of intimacy, love and knowledge. The invisible God becomes incredibly personal in the birth of Jesus.

Pause for thought

Jesus is always by our side in a personal way, and this should have a transforming influence on our daily living. He has an intimate knowledge of the small details of our lives and by the power of the Holy Spirit He wants this close relationship to be sensed by those we meet today. In Scripture, the closeness of Jesus in the life of the believer is likened to the smell of a fragrant perfume. It can convey the knowledge of the good news found in Jesus Christ (2 Cor. 2:14–16).

Prayer for today

Breathe on me Holy Spirit,
Cleanse and renew me.
May the living presence of Jesus so shine through my life today
That the fragrance of the gospel will bring joy to all I meet.
To the glory of Jesus' name.
Amen

Reflection

My wife and I have a friend who is a midwife. One day she was visiting an expectant mother who lived in an isolated house in a rural area. While she was there, the mother began to give birth and complications developed. The midwife came out of the bedroom to phone for some backup, but it became plain that any medical support was at least an hour away.

Our friend said that she offered up an 'arrow prayer' and the answer was immediate. She heard God saying to her, 'I will be your hands and mind in this delivery room.' She returned to the mother and in spite of the complications, the baby was safely delivered. Her testimony was that God was by her side when she needed Him most.

Suggestion for group activity – Week Four

Joy to the streets!
The purpose of this project is to provide Christmas hampers for the poorest in the community where you live. This project might involve just your house group but ideally the whole church family should be involved.

1. From your own contacts as a church, identify the most needy families in your community. In addition, approach local health visitors or community agencies, explaining that you are preparing Christmas hampers, and asking if they would appreciate receiving some to distribute among the poorest families they know.

2. Seek financial support from your church and invite gifts of money from individuals to the Christmas hamper project. Where appropriate, seek support from the local business community.

3. Having budgeted how many hampers you can prepare, purchase gifts of food appropriate to Christmas and convene a time in early December when as a group you pack and prepare the hampers. Include in the hamper a copy of either J. John's *What's the Point of Christmas?* (Oxford: Lion Hudson, 2004) or Jeff Lucas' *Infinite Hope* (Worthing: Christian Publicity Organisation, 2008).

4. Plan that the hampers will be distributed sometime between 22 and 24 December.

1. Stephen Hawking, *A Brief History of Time* (London: Bantam Books, 1998) p.13.
2. Christopher J. Ellis and Myra Blyth for the Baptist Union of Great Britain, *Gathering for Worship: Patterns and Prayers for the Community of Disciples* (Norwich: Canterbury Press, 2005) p.355. Used by permission.
3. Jane Williams, *Approaching Christmas* (Oxford: Lion Hudson, 2005) p.110.
4. Philips Brooks (1835–1893), extract from 'O Little Town of Bethlehem'.
5. James Montgomery Boice, *Foundations of the Christian Faith* (Leicester: Inter-Varsity Press, 1986) p.407.
6. Arthur Bennett, extract from 'The Gift of Gifts', *The Valley of Vision: A collection of Puritan Prayers and Devotions* (Edinburgh: The Banner of Truth Trust, 1975) p.16. Used by permission. www.banneroftruth.co.uk
7. Philip Yancey, *Reaching for the Invisible God* (Grand Rapids: Zondervan, 2000) p.10.
8. J.I. Packer, *Knowing God* (London: Hodder and Stoughton, 1973) p.46.

Gifts of Joy

Soon the Christmas decorations will be taken down and stored away for another year. When Christmas comes to an end there can be the feeling that the celebration is over. Epiphany, however, gives us the opportunity to reflect on the lessons we have learned through Advent.

Epiphany is celebrated in different ways throughout the world Church. One old tradition says three wonders mark this holy season: the revelation to the Magi of Jesus the Light of the whole world; the baptism of Jesus and the commencement of His ministry; the first sign when Jesus turned water into wine and revealed His glory.

Our focus in the final week of this Advent book will be to consider the latecomers to the stable of Jesus. The Wise Men have something to teach us about those who live on the edge of the Church.

Our final meditation of the old year is a reminder that the best response to the greatest gift is the daily gift of a life of service.

Seek and you will find

Bible passage
Matthew 2:1–12

Research into family trees is a popular pastime for many. Our family has researchers who have delved into the long (and *mostly* venerable!) history of the Coffey tribe. Like most families we have luminaries who have succeeded and also those who could make the front page of the Sunday tabloids!

Matthew commences his Gospel with the family tree of Jesus. The luminaries are there – Abraham the father of the Jewish nation and David the king *par excellence*. But the recurring theme running through this family tree is that God's gospel is good news for outsiders as well as insiders. The least likely are included.

Chapter 2 opens with the same theme. Out of the blue ride some foreigners (Matt. 2:1–2). They had been reading the stars and had made a long adventurous journey seeking more information from those who know their Bible.

At the time of Jesus' birth there was huge interest in astrology. When something startling happened in the astronomical world it was interpreted as God doing something new in the universe. Jewish people remembered the prophecy that 'A star will come out of Jacob; a sceptre will rise out of Israel' (Num. 24:17). The star that the Wise Men followed may have looked to them like a comet behaving in an unusual way, with its tail pointing downward over Bethlehem.

The baby lying in the manger was Jewish, but soon Gentiles would come streaming into the Church. Matthew would have seen the arrival of the visitors from the east as a fulfilment of Isaiah's vision that 'Nations will come to your light, and kings to the brightness of your dawn' (Isa. 60:3). This could explain why he concludes his

Gospel with Jesus' commission for the spreading of the good news to the whole world (Matt. 28:18–20). The Magi gathering at the cradle is a symbolic representation of the world coming to know of Jesus.

Pause for thought
The visitors from the east symbolise the core of the missionary message of the Bible: Whatever your culture, every knee is invited to bow at Jesus' feet. Whatever your kingdom, this is the true King to whom we bow the knee.

Prayer for today
Lord Jesus
You are the Light of the whole world
Your love and grace extend to all people
Thank You that there is no one beyond the reach
of Your redeeming love
Show me how I can share this love in my own
community today
For your name's sake
Amen

Reflection
Who are the wise men and women who are seeking Jesus today? Remember some of them will be in your circle of friends and acquaintances. They may consider themselves outsiders but are searching for a way to fulfil their spiritual quest. Are you alert for their questions? Are you prepared to be non-judgmental concerning their faith journey thus far? Will you accept them as openly as the Wise Men were welcomed at the manger of Jesus?

30 Dec

Knock and the stable door will open

Bible passage
Matthew 2:3–8

In a survey conducted amongst a sample of students in England, 100 per cent knew their star sign, 70 per cent read their horoscopes regularly and 85 per cent agreed that the description of their birth sign described their personality.

The late Princess Diana said her grandmother was looking after her in the spirit world and had attempted to contact her through a clairvoyant. She regularly visited her astrologer, and according to her close friends did not have a conventional belief in God, but was constantly seeking an explanation for life's endless cycle of chaos, pain and drama.

As a Christian, I don't consult any astrological charts so I find it incredible that God spoke to the Wise Men in their eastern star-gazing culture.

Matthew takes us on a journey 1,000 miles east of Bethlehem to an area which now makes up modern-day Iran and Iraq. The people in this region had no history of being big friends with God, but they were open-minded and seeking. God met them where they were. He came to their world.

God speaks to them in ways they can understand. These Wise Men live in a world of flaky religion based on astrology, astronomy, Middle East politics and a dash of Bible knowledge. God enters this world and draws them in to the Jesus story through the movement of a star. But remember, there is more to the story than the star.

This is the full sequence of what happened to the Wise Men: God spoke to them in creation when they saw a configuration in the stars (Matt. 2:2); God spoke to them through the Bible when the chief priests and teachers of the law indicated Bethlehem was the birthplace of the promised Messiah (vv.5–6); God spoke to them in Jesus, as when they met Him they bowed down and worshipped Him (v.11).

F.D. Bruner summarises these stages of the journey for all who are seeking Jesus:

God's revelation in nature raises the question and begins
the quest;
God's revelation in Scriptures gives the answer and directs
the quest to the goal;
God's revelation in Christ – the goal – satisfies the quest.[1]

Pause for thought
We need to find ways of relating in the bewildering spirituality of our
times. We know the ultimate goal is for people to meet Jesus, so we
need to remember the early stages of the journey and observe how
God speaks to seekers.

It is the lesson of the Magi. Knock and the stable door will open.

Prayer for today
Star child,
wanted and welcomed by the humble,
hated and hounded by power-seekers;
refuge and refugee,
we love you![2]

Reflection
How far are you prepared to travel to meet a friend where they are
spiritually? Sometimes people need that personal encouragement to
recognise that God is inviting them to knock at the stable door and
meet Jesus.

31 Dec

A fistful of wrong notes

Bible passages
Matthew 2:9–12; Romans 12:1–3

I once read an interview with the concert pianist Daniel Barenboim.
He said in the interview, 'Every concert I've finished with the
knowledge I've played a fistful of wrong notes.'[3]

This is the last day of the old year and our Advent journey is drawing to a close. As I look back on the year I am aware that most days I played 'a fistful of wrong notes'. I made the wrong choices, I chose inappropriate words, I rushed to judgments on people, I ploughed ahead with enthusiasm for my human plans, I lived in a narrow world of my own interests.

How do we bridge the gap between the good that God intends for our lives and that 'fistful of wrong notes?' The answer is to simply give your best – which is what the Wise Men did. When they saw Jesus they bowed down, worshipped and presented their gifts (Matt. 2:11).

Gold is the gift you present to a king, incense was in constant use by the priests in the Temple, myrrh was used to embalm the dead. The gifts of these Wise Men are an amazing revelation of the true significance of the baby Jesus. Jesus is the King who deserves the gold of our lives, the best for Him who is simply the best; Jesus is the Priest who makes ultimate reconciliation possible between God and human beings; Jesus is the Saviour born to die, and by His loving sacrifice we have forgiveness of sins.

Each one of us can offer the gift of our body in a life of service in the world (Rom. 12:1; Heb. 13:15; 1 Pet. 2:5). We have been purchased at a great price – the precious blood Christ shed on the cross. Our lives are no longer our own (1 Cor. 6:19–20).

Each day, as an act of spiritual worship, we can offer to God the best for His service. The phrase 'spiritual worship' indicates a mind and a heart that are fully engaged. Thinking worshippers avoid worldly patterns of service – instead they go with the grain of God's work of transformation taking place in their lives (Rom. 12:2).

Pause for thought
Compare Mark 9:2 and 2 Corinthians 3:18 and see the links between the words 'transfigure' and 'transform'. The former passage concerns the transfiguration of Jesus ('a complete change came over Jesus'). The latter passage concerns the transformation of the Christian ('transformed into His likeness'). By stages God pledges to deal with our 'fistful of wrong notes'.

Prayer for today

May the peace of the Lord Christ go with you,
wherever he may send you.
May he guide you through the wilderness,
protect you through the storm.
May he bring you home rejoicing
at the wonders he has shown you.
May he bring you home rejoicing
once again into our doors.[4]

Reflection

It's a worthwhile exercise to reflect on the gifts you have offered to the Lord recently.

Has He received the gift of your quality time? Are there talents that have been under-employed which could be useful for His kingdom? Is there a gift of money that could bring a blessing to another Christian or advance a mission project?

Offer the Lord your treasured gifts of time, talents and possessions, and be bold enough to ask Him for a new adventure!

Suggestion for group activity – Week Five

Giving and receiving

Prepare a New Year's Eve gathering based around the theme of gifts. Send out invitations, asking guests to bring with them an inexpensive wrapped gift. Ask each person not to tell anyone what is in his or her parcel.

The early part of the evening gathering can be a social time, with games, food and drink. If you have twelve to fifteen guests you will need to start the latter part of the evening around 10.30pm.

Have a hat ready with small numbered cards in it – one for each person there. At the appropriate time in the evening, place all the parcels people have brought in the middle of the room. Invite each guest to draw a number from the hat. Ask the person with No.1 to choose a parcel and unwrap it.

The person with No.2 can either choose an unwrapped gift or choose to take the gift already opened (No.1). If the person chooses to take gift No.1, the original recipient takes another gift from the pile.

The game proceeds with the same rules – people can choose either an unwrapped gift or one already opened. With the last player and all parcels opened, the game ends.

Take a short break and prepare a table with a lighted candle at the centre and unlit tea lights around the base of the candle. Invite someone to give a brief meditation on the blessing of giving and receiving.

Each person in the group is then invited to light a tea light from the central candle. Encourage the guests to give thanks to God as they light the candles, for 'a gift' which has blessed them during the old year, and to make a commitment to shine the light of their own gifts in a specific place during the New Year.

Have a time of open prayer, and towards midnight conclude by saying the Lord's Prayer together.

1. Frederick Dale Bruner, *Matthew, Volume 1, The Christbook, Matthew 1–12* (Dallas: Word, 1987) p.44.
2. Christopher J. Ellis and Myra Blyth for the Baptist Union of Great Britain, 'Devotion and praise for Epiphany', *Gathering for Worship: Patterns and Prayers for the Community of Disciples* (Norwich: Canterbury Press, 2005) p.364. Used by permission.
3. Laura Barnett, 'Portrait of the artist' interview, *Guardian* newspaper (29 January 2008) p.29.
4. Peter Sutcliffe, 'The Blessing' from The Northumbria Community's, *Celtic Daily Prayer* (London: HarperCollins, 2000) p.19. Used by permission.

National Distributors

UK: (and countries not listed below)
CWR, Waverley Abbey House, Waverley Lane, Farnham, Surrey GU9 8EP.
Tel: (01252) 784700 Outside UK (44) 1252 784700

AUSTRALIA: CMC Australasia, PO Box 519, Belmont, Victoria 3216.
Tel: (03) 5241 3288 Fax: (03) 5241 3290

CANADA: David C Cook Distribution Canada, PO Box 98, 55 Woodslee Avenue, Paris, Ontario N3L 3E5.
Tel: 1800 263 2664

GHANA: Challenge Enterprises of Ghana, PO Box 5723, Accra.
Tel: (021) 222437/223249 Fax: (021) 226227

HONG KONG: Cross Communications Ltd, 1/F, 562A Nathan Road, Kowloon.
Tel: 2780 1188 Fax: 2770 6229

INDIA: Crystal Communications, 10-3-18/4/1, East Marredpalli, Secunderabad – 500026, Andhra Pradesh.
Tel/Fax: (040) 27737145

KENYA: Keswick Books and Gifts Ltd, PO Box 10242, Nairobi.
Tel: (02) 331692/226047 Fax: (02) 728557

MALAYSIA: Salvation Book Centre (M) Sdn Bhd, 23 Jalan SS 2/64, 47300 Petaling Jaya, Selangor.
Tel: (03) 78766411/78766797 Fax: (03) 78757066/78756360

NEW ZEALAND: CMC Australasia, PO Box 303298, North Harbour, Auckland 0751.
Tel: 0800 449 408 Fax: 0800 449 049

NIGERIA: FBFM, Helen Baugh House, 96 St Finbarr's College Road, Akoka, Lagos.
Tel: (01) 7747429/4700218/825775/827264

PHILIPPINES: OMF Literature Inc, 776 Boni Avenue, Mandaluyong City.
Tel: (02) 531 2183 Fax: (02) 531 1960

SINGAPORE: Alby Commercial Enterprises Pte Ltd, 95 Kallang Avenue #04-00, AIS Industrial Building, 339420.
Tel: (65) 629 27238 Fax: (65) 629 27235

SOUTH AFRICA: Struik Christian Books, 80 MacKenzie Street, PO Box 1144, Cape Town 8000.
Tel: (021) 462 4360 Fax: (021) 461 3612

SRI LANKA: Christombu Publications (Pvt) Ltd, Bartleet House, 65 Braybrooke Place, Colombo 2.
Tel: (9411) 2421073/2447665

TANZANIA: CLC Christian Book Centre, PO Box 1384, Mkwepu Street, Dar es Salaam.
Tel/Fax: (022) 2119439

USA: David C Cook Distribution Canada, PO Box 98, 55 Woodslee Avenue, Paris, Ontario N3L 3E5, Canada.
Tel: 1800 263 2664

ZIMBABWE: Word of Life Books (Pvt) Ltd, Christian Media Centre, 8 Aberdeen Road, Avondale, PO Box A480
Avondale, Harare.
Tel: (04) 333355 or 091301188

For email addresses, visit the CWR website: www.cwr.org.uk

CWR is a Registered Charity - Number 294387

CWR is a Limited Company registered in England - Registration Number 1990308

Sit at Jesus' feet and learn from Him this Lent

This Lent, gain a deeper understanding of the life and teaching of Christ and the meaning of His sacrifice on the cross with these studies in John 14–17 which will help you to:

- Spend time with Jesus, learning from Him and getting closer to Him
- Grapple with eternal truths that are difficult to grasp
- See the big picture of God's salvation plan and gain an eternal perspective.

With opening icebreakers, suggested prayers and discussion starters, this guide is ideal for both individual and small-group study.

The Time Has Come
by Beryl Adamsbaum
84-page, A5 booklet
ISBN: 978-1-85345-486-8
Only £5.99

Journey through the Bible, as it happened, in a year

Your confidence in the Bible will increase as you see how it forms a single, comprehensive story across the centuries. This thrilling voyage of discovery through God's Word includes:

- Charts, maps, illustrations and diagrams that will enhance your understanding of the Bible's big story and biblical times
- A timeline across each page to keep every event in context for you
- Devotional thoughts to help you apply each day's reading
- The full text of the flowing, contemporary Holman Christian Standard translation, divided into manageable daily portions in chronological order.

Reference Book of the Year 2008 – UK Christian Booksellers

Cover to Cover Complete
by Selwyn Hughes and Trevor J. Partridge
1,632-page hardback
ISBN: 978-1-85345-433-2
Only £19.99

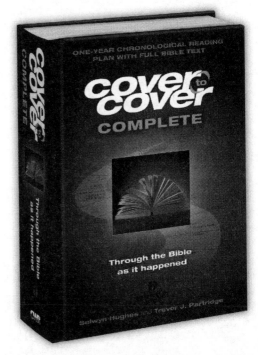